POETRY RIVALS'
COLLECTION 2009

LYRICAL WINDS

Edited by Lisa Adlam

forward press

First published in Great Britain in 2009 by:
Forward Press
Remus House
Coltsfoot Drive
Peterborough
PE2 9JX
Telephone: 01733 890099
Website: www.forwardpress.co.uk

FOREWORD

Poetry Rivals 2009 was one of the biggest and most prestigious poetry competitions ever held by Forward Press, and a talent contest like no other.

Poets of all ages and from all corners of the globe were invited to write a poem that stood out from the rest - a poem that showed true creative talent.

This vast collection, chosen by the Forward Press editors, is the result. I'm sure you'll agree that the diversity and richness of the poetry included is unique - and a reflection of the inspiration to be found in modern day poetry.

As well as providing an exciting opportunity for poets to showcase their creativity, Poetry Rivals has given today's poetry a public platform to be showcased and rewarded, as it deserves.

CONTENTS

THE POEMS

WELCOME TO THE FRAY

One thing we know, one thing we all see
is an adult's proud bearing melt in a new babe's eyes,
the mask it drops and the joy it springs.

Each little face, each smile and frown
brings a sprinkling of joy with an icing of hope,
hope for the future, for little eyes burning so bright.

Small hands rest on ours, soft and pale,
wisps of hair and eyes of wonder,
smiles to light the world and cries to shatter the drums.

One child is a blessing and two double so,
one child changes your world,
two recreate your world.

Babes' eyes, brown and blue,
reflect the future, potential of the new,
wonder and joy for all who'd see them.

Today's a day to dream of what could be,
a time to welcome to the fray,
Jack and Kali as they make their way.

Paul Taylor

WORDS

Rising to consciousness is poetry's mysterious gift,
The epiphany of a word,
Input of brilliance, that resonates of clarity,
Transcending, becoming, moulding the shape of a confirmation,
Of understanding,
Of a sudden, articulate and immediate.
A wonder of serendipity and its essence of inner joy,
Indescribable, a whiff of its aura.
Of no firm shape or explanation,
No delineation that explains its all.
But it's there.

Ray Dite

ORBIT

The world spins.
I see it through a zoetrope,
Only jarring glimpses of it reaching me.
A slideshow of a place
Full of smiling, happy people
I neither can nor want to be like.
I cannot touch this Technicolor paradise.
My world is dark;
A labyrinthine corner;
A cavernous cage.
Empty. Filled with shadows
Silently screaming at me,
Bursting my eardrums,
Beating the inside of my skull
With a rhythm as mad and chaotic
As my incoherent babbling thoughts.
I claw at the walls for something to do.
It should hurt but I feel nothing,
I carry on to see if I will bleed.
Am I real? Am I human? Am I hollow?
I don't know. I am lost,
Wandering through the murky paths of my world,
Tendrils of fog grasping my wrists and ankles
Pulling me back, pulling me down, pulling me deeper,
Clouding my vision in a sea of grey.
The mist teases me,
Shows me shapes, glimpses of colour,
Echoes of distant voices and laughter,
Making me think I'm almost there,
I can almost touch it,
Soon I can be it,
Normality is within reach!
But all is dark. All is fog.
The shapes disappear, the sounds fade away.
The fog lifts, I'm bobbing gently up and down
In my little world out in open water.
The tide of life has taken me
Far beyond the point of safe return.
My cheeks are glistening but my eyes are dry;
The salt has temporarily healed my wounds.
Lying back, looking at the sky.

The waves rise up on all sides,
Rocking me, comforting me,
Reaching for the clouds, obscuring my view,
Taking me back to my labyrinth,
Taking me home.
I reach for the toy that lies beside me,
My link to the outside.
I pick it up and give it a twirl.
Peeking through it I can see all.
The world spins.

Samantha Baker

THE GUILTY

Unpick the stitches, pull out the thread
The fabric sewn is almost spared
But tiny perforations mark the cloth
Where needle pierced apart and
Broke the tightly garment woven
The line still traceable
Though unspoken.
Clear your conscience, quell the flood
Of unwanted thoughts, of blood, of mud
Collect up the pieces
Glue back the vase
Prop up the dead
Rebuild the façade
Living in constant fear
The damage done may reappear
A ghostly vision always present
Indelibly marked
Never driven far
From the mind's
Inescapable prison.

Lara Charles

UNTITLED

Oooooooohhhh
you missed me wearing my suit!
I hardly ever wear my suit
thank God!
We don't ever want to go down there again.

Pages and pages
the flying monkeys and the tiger rain still falls on the tiger people
and that, scuttles and shadows away the joys in life and
the person stands hidden beneath the other person . . .

or behind their demanding silver sheen

or take it all away I will drink my bottle
my bottle will take it all away.

Now do you want some shine, child?
To cancel all the dreams, the silver machines and the
                                                  elephant touch?

Turn your key in my lock for the first time
turn it forever? Your turn?

Well. We've got it here to talk about,
get your identity,
                                        the soul without
      and the soul within.

Orange moon come up to me,   sing.
Kiss me
now
my love.

                                        Elephants
                                          sing.

Always bright colours,
brightest reds for my anger and passion
my anger for protection,
                      creation, personalities of the sub-order
                      shadow me my true love, kissed once,
just beneath the surface, all rains,
                      keeping me from my shadow . . . Damage

shadow
shadow

kiss me
kiss me
kiss me
kiss me
kiss me
kiss me
kiss me
kiss me
kiss me

I want to kiss me . . .
                    I want you to kiss me . . .

Graham Brodie

MESSING ABOUT ON THE RIVER

Right bank lines
of daisies brown
middled white petalled bit
flat and heavy headed
coming together
in wind to
lick half-brown rocks
emphasising green mat-
like grass radiating
in all directions as if
painted to blend
into meadows, hills, the mist
swirling thickly, clinging
and forest-climbing
dwindling before me
somewhere into
dark sky-blue circles
lost in the white swell.

Doreen King

HAPPINESS

What is this fleeting thing called happiness?
It comes and goes and is as transient
As rainbows in the sky with summer rain
Or clouds across the moon.

For happiness is like a precious jewel
Suspended, glowing, in its own pure light.
It shines amid the gloom of humdrum life.
Stretch out your hands to clasp
And hold it close, and cherish it, and wish
That time would cease its motion evermore-
The jewel cradled for eternity.
But such will not endure.

Oh, cast your eyes across to war-torn lands,
And search the depths of human misery.
Take pity on the gaunt and weeping child.
Shall we be happy still?
For happiness is likened to a star
Which, when our cares diminish, fade and die,
Appears as a tiny gleam,
Then grows and warms us with a radiance divine.
We'll hold it fast, this bright exquisite star
And build a fortress round it in our hearts
Lest some dark thing creeps in to steal its light.
'Tis all in vain.

Alas! Too quickly passes happiness.
The jewel shatters, and the star is dimmed,
Lost in the darkness of encroaching storms.
Maybe, elusive happiness - of such fragility -
Endures in quiet contentment,
But not in ecstasy.

Jean M Jackson

THE STORM CONCERTO

Watching through the window
Clothes lines swaying
In unison to the wind's waltz
Bushes bowing in line
Trees swaying in time
To nature's rhapsody
Raindrops pitter-pattering
Their rhythm against the window

Even cats stay hidden
When nature's orchestra
Plays its overture
The white plastic bag
Flaps seagull-like
Amidst the turbulent air
As if guided by an invisible hand

I can almost see
The drummers of the band
Waves pounding against rocks
Demonstrating nature's pervasive force
Again the wind section
Returns to play

The howl and whine
Joining forces with the clashing
Of doors and gates
The creak of rafters
All playing their own part
In nature's thunderous
Cacophony of sound . . .

F Knowles

WHO AM I?

What do you see when you look at me?
Do you judge by my race - or by my face?
Am I much too tall or very small?
Am I fat or thin - do I frown or grin?
Am I happy or sad or good or bad?
As you see me go - am I fast or slow?
Go on - tell me - I want to know!
But listen, my friend, have you ever thought
That what you see may be what I'm not?
For inside me are many things:
Hopes, ideas, expectations and dreams.
I've lived a life that would fill a book
So maybe you should take another look.
There's another me that you cannot see
And I need to release it and set it free.
But maybe the fault is partly mine
As I keep it hidden so much of the time.
I long to let folks take a peek inside
But most of the time I just want to hide
All of my longings, desires and thoughts
In case what you think of me won't be a lot.
But there's one I can talk to without any fear,
He does not condemn and I know He will hear
All of the innermost thoughts of my heart,
And tells me His presence will never depart.
He's taken my sins and He's washed them away
And promised to take me to see Him one day,
Then all of this outer façade that you see
Will change to be like Him, 'What joy that will be'.
So please - take a look at the innermost part
When you look at me,
'Cause that is my heart.

Meta Hester

THE POET

Deep inside,
Where the poetry grows,
Blossoms, expands,
Explodes!
Taking on a life of its own,
Flooding out,
Ripping down dams,
Leaving no doubt.
It destroys in its wake
People, trees, nature, life,
All are as nothing,
All are in strife.
Deep down below,
The places we fear to go,
Darkness creeps within,
Hiding all we don't want to know,
Or think.
Thoughts on the tide,
Sharp as razors, cut with knives.
Always there inside.
Waiting for the break,
When the poetry lets out,
Comes with quiet,
Comes with shout,
It won't let go,
Won't let you sleep,
Till pen on paper
Like snails' trails creep.
It has a purpose,
The voice gives wing,
Without words
There is no meaning.

Trudi Webber

ANGEL

Angel, you who are silent and wise,
Angel, you who are mine
To guide me through my trials and troubles,
To get me through my desperate times.

Angel, you who are silent and wise,
A secret witness throughout my life,
I lean my head upon your shoulder,
I find my resting space

That lies hidden deep within me,
Through your silent, sweet embrace.

Angel, you who give me shelter
From both sorrow and from fear,
Angel, you who stand beside me
Always trusting, always there.

Because you are my silent angel,
You grant me freedom from my fear,
You take the seeds to their succession,
Always higher,
Always freer,
Always deeper,
Always newer,
Never ending,
Never stopping,
Always changing,
Always growing,
Helping me to have desire,
Helping me to fly much higher.

Constantly,
You do stand by me,
Perfection and ability,
That lies dormant deep within us
Grows by your sincerity

Nourished by your sweet affection,
We rise to levels of perfection,
That we never would have imagined

Without your presence,
Without your prayers,
Without your kindness,

Without your grace,

Without the sacred space created
By your silent, sweet embrace.

Echoes of those huge successes,
Triumphs of that jubilee,
Enters my heart by your presence,
From here to the Eternity,
You know my full propensity,

Through you I reach my destiny.

Favourite of the masters
Saving the masses from disasters,
Guiding the crowds on the pathways,
Through the jungles and the mountains,
In the cities and the free space
Forward home
To understanding
Our brilliant nature,
Now demanding,
Craving, wanting education,
We keep on moving,
Keep on changing,
Constant change and new improvement,
Taking all to higher levels,
You are an assistant on the stairways,
Up, up, up to constant action,
Constant passion and compassion,
Always giving and receiving,
Never stopping,
Not deceiving.

Leading us to higher ground
With new visions and ambitions,
Always daring and profound,
Make a fresh and new beginning,
A vision of a better place,
Let's keep playing,
Love is here, love is there and all around,
A new place,
A new beginning,
Are you willing, are you ready,
Make commitment,
Take command,
For our children,

For the future,
A resting place,
A safer ground.
For your children,
For our future,
A safer place to rest and play.
Do not worry,
Do not hurry,
Now is now and you've been found,
Step up now to newer levels,

Always daring and profound.

Gently, you lead us to forgiveness,
Softly, you help us to release
The pain and hurt
That did come our way

And froze our hearts like a disease.

With ease,
Let go now,
Keep on moving,
Find your freedom,
Keep improving,
Set yourself free,
Escape the prison,

Let go, let go and feel the peace.

I declare my love for you, my angel,
My angel of comfort,
My angel of light,
I declare my love for you, my angel,

I kneel before you,
I give up pride,
I need, I need you, oh so badly,
I need your guidance and your grace,
I need your smile and your attention,

The love that shows upon your face.

All is feeling, all is presence
And rests inside your sweet embrace.

Please do not hide yourself from me;
I need to see you face to face.

Keys to the locks of the deepest chambers,

The deepest chambers of our hearts
Are in your hand and freely giving,
Say yes to take
And open the doors of freedom and compassion,
The doors of hearts and feel the passion,
The love, which flows just like a river,
Drives us further,
Sets us freer,
Newer, newer, new beginnings,
Take a stand and find a passion,
A love so deep and quite old-fashioned,
The deepest secret,
The greatest passion is there within your sweet embrace.

Luckily, I came across you,
The passion of living, and the passion of life,
All these feelings and emotions

Supported by your sweet embrace.

Over the years to come you witness
Transformation of many millions,
Turning rags into riches,
Silently present to hear their wishes,
Setting out on new, new journeys
With the goal of soon becoming
Divinely inspired beings,
Present there for others seeing
What they want and what they aim for,
See the target and shoot the arrow,
Become a guide of silent being,
Gently guiding,
Gently caring,
With great affection,
Always sharing,
Nourish,
Give and gently care,
Knowing truly the distinction:

'God, help those who help themselves.'

You are the support of the uneducated,
Those who trust your gentle push.

You are the star, angel of perfection,
In a team of divine succession,
Helping them ignite their fire,

Find their passions and desires,
Make a stand and take a chance,

Teaching the masses to deal with their fears.

Your team is tight;
Their spirit is high
In guiding all others
To relish their high.

Angel, you would never give up on me,
In a million years to come.

Because you
Are always
There for someone,
Someone is always
There for you.

Indupati Monk

UNTITLED

She hunts on the outskirts.
On the one hand there is Future.
There is life beyond the moment
and there is the promise of contentment.
Some seek bliss.
But those that dream awake, know better.

She hunts on the outskirts.
On the one hand there is Nothing.
There is fog about the conscience
and there is the promise of destruction.
Some seek loss.
But those that scream asleep, know better.

Molly Garner

WHEN THE BATTLE CRIES DIE

Look at me, my nameless friend,
Does this really have to be the end
Of your time on this earth - your unique life
For mindless hatred; sickening strife, -
And arrogance of senseless thought,
In the midst of a self-destructing war.

Talk to me, my nameless friend,
And listen to the wish I send.
Seize not my life, but take my reaching hand,
Let shameful weapons wane upon the land.
I cannot watch you slain in heartless death.
I *will* not watch you take your final breath.

Come to me, my nameless friend
And let's no longer both defend
This venomous line that divides both you and I,
And reflects in the tears of your fearful eyes.
For I feel your heart as you long to be free.
Cross the line and unite in our humanity.

Here you are, my nameless friend,
Face to face at last, we stand.
The time to swallow remorse and falsified pride,
And live like true brothers in strength, side by side.
For the conflict and battle has gone between us,
And I know that in me, you have given your trust.

Stay with me, dear friend
And pray the world of wars will end.
Maybe one day, the bloodied rages will cease,
With real understanding, patience and peace.
Until then, we continue to ask ourselves why,
And dream for the day when the battle cries die . . .

Lynda Ann Green

MY FENG SHUI LOVER (FROM THE LINCOLNSHIRE FENS)

A previous lover had told you
you were a 'loose cannon' and so
you asked me, your latest lover,
what it meant.
Admiring his veracity and candour,
abandoning tact, sounding like a dictionary
but pleased to get it off my chest,
I replied,
'You have an erratic capacity
for doing a bloke's head in.'

And I meant it too,
sadly,
but nice to know - I wasn't the first.

You were into all this 'alternative' stuff,
I bet you kept in business the local tech:
Feng shui, aromatherapy, t'ai chi,
metaphysical basket making,
and your CD collection portrayed all,
at the same time revealing - the 'split' in you,
the 'loose cannon' for
'Sacred Native American 19th Century Chanting Music'
nestled firmly against
'Madonna's Greatest Hits',
and that was the contradiction that messed you up,
the outsider versus the teenybopper;
I was placed, feng shui-style, in the middle,
In the crossfire of your insensitivity.

Yes, you always 'did my head in' as they say,
'expert' at arranging the brain cells,
unfortunately like a bull in a china shop,
certainly not with therapeutic skill,
and so you always left me not knowing
my ying from my yang.
The doorbell to your flat brought no reply
when often you told me you'd definitely be in,
and every blow I took
landed squarely upon my chin,
except one day as you practised t'ai chi

you accidentally thumbed me in the eye
and reached excitedly for your aromatherapy case;
taking out the perfumed tea tree with eucalyptus
(at least it wasn't mace)
you bore down upon me
claiming the smell was 'nice';
unusually for me, I refused your advance:
the shock must have broken the romantic trance.

Lying in bed together, next to you and your Victorian
teddy bear, (bought from 'Past Times'),
me wooing you like only an outsider can,
you would suddenly become unhappy
with the bedroom's ying and yang,
and leaping out of bed
carefully nudge that framed picture of your mother
or relocate the desk diary
containing details of your past lovers.
But your 'alternative' ways didn't make you a 'raver',
sad to say,
only a woman who raved,
perhaps we all saw you as our sexual saviour;
but in fact you often treated me
as if you were doing me a favour -
my feng shui lover, my 'loose cannon' love.

And yet I often miss you now,
the philosopher in me drawn to your wacky ways,
whereas the truth really was
you were a well-disguised wrecking-ball
as others too had found, by their fall,
but such are the destructive devices of a devious Fate.
Yes, everything had to be in the right place
but lovers were best left disorganised and roughly arranged;
they could fend for themselves in this cruel world
whereas those pretty shapes of healing crystal would not.

Yet amidst all your bottles of wisdom,
of aromatherapeutic oils,
your ying and yang gravitas,
the t'ai chi balletic grace,
there was one thing you never did realise:
that when it came to loving you
my heart was always
in the right place.

Ty Dalby

DESTINY UNKNOWN

Love me as you loved me once,
    A million years ago,
    Or so it seems,
Voice the words I long to hear,
    Recapture vanished dreams.

Return to days of shared content,
    Our destiny unknown,
    Regard each dying ember,
Gladden my heart with a promise,
    Make bright our grey December.

Deepest thoughts remain untold,
    Countless words unsaid,
    I know not why,
Rekindle then the flame of love,
    Let love not pass us by.

Joan Armstead

LANDFILL

Broiling, mewling gulls land and snatch their fill,
Lured from habitat by prodigious waste.
In a sea of discarded goods and chattels
Lie split bags of food in glutinous paste.

Up high the driver in his yellow cab
Lifts and shifts the detritus of our lives.
There a doll that once attended picnics,
Close by the paper plates and plastic knives.

Is there treasure amongst this retching smell?
Soon buried deep the ring that was not lost
But thrown, a discarded token of love.
Symbolic place of warmth that's cooled to frost.

Pamela Boal

THE CHAMELEON

Tonight I thought again of the chameleon
that you brought back like a trophy.
By chance you had found it
by the side of the road.
It was dying, you said,
but like a child I was filled
with the drama of its arrival,
convinced that we could save it.
I had never seen one before,
The perfect smallness of its form.
I thought it would be bigger somehow,
like an iguana.
We placed it on the low wall,
on its side in white dust,
no longer able to stand.
We watched its breathing
quick and small.
Its magnificent turning eye,
still turning.
Its tail
coiled round
unable to cling to branch,
nor to anything, save itself.
Its four tiny feet,
opposable toes, half-curled,
small beginnings of an unmade grasp.
We tried to revive it with water -
the futile drip of the hose.
And as your hand left mine
I watched its colour
change
from the brown of its arrival
to the white of surrender
or a last camouflage
against the bleached pallor of stones?
Two complete colours
in the space of one skin.

Alison Armstrong

19

ENIGMATIC WHISPERS

Softly, stealthily, do the images appear.
Unbidden, but welcomed by the somniferous soul.
A gentle breeze that carries the mocking cry of indigenous seabirds
And the fragrance of wood smoke, down the passages of time.
Not only acts as a tantalising trigger for the senses,
But also forms a portal through which one can enter this sphere.
To become acutely aware, deliciously conscious, of the
riches of this realm.

Certain aspects of this mirage always remain the same.
The ancient steps, the swirling mists, the brooding shadows
of archaic buildings.
All constants on an ever-changing canvas of illusion and fantasy.
But know that beyond these invariable markers
Lay the promise of one's greatest desires.
Your guide awaits, with proffered hand, to lead you on your way.
To take you to the boundaries of your salaciousness.

So come - for beyond the billowing veil lies this enticing world.
See contained in the eyes of your guide, fathomless depths
of feeling.
Recognise the mighty ocean that lies within. Turbulent,
pulsating, surging.
Longing to send thunderous waves crashing into the cavernous
orifices of the waiting shore.
Lie comfortably disrobed upon a sweet, heady-scented bed
of rose petals.
Have those imperious globes hungrily devour your very essence.
Know that without even being touched, you can achieve the
fullness of your ardour.

Partake then in the full gloriousness of the feast.
Feed ravenously upon the way in which it is presented.
Take in the opulent appearance of the bounty before you.
Sample all the delicacies on this abundant platter of
captivating fascination.
Tempt, tease and coax the rare exotic fruits to yield of
their contents.
For within the soft, succulent, fleshy skin hides the sweetest juice,
A libation produced to quench the most insatiable of thirsts.

Join in the rhythmic age old dance of yin and yang.
Savour the exquisite pleasure of oleaginous flesh caressing
oleaginous flesh,
Seeming to glow in the flickering light of a myriad of tiny
candle flames.
Luxuriate in the delicately musky aroma that permeates
the atmosphere.
Willingly welcome these hedonistic sensations into your psyche.
Allow the sumptuous decadence of the moment to release you,
From a state of fierce rigidity into a state of delightful flaccidity.

Ah but alas, no amount of yearning can hold the spirit forever
in this realm.
The awareness of time trickles through the nebulous blanket
of this sanctuary.
Shards of indistinct light creep tentatively from the chinks
appearing in the veil,
And subtle nuances of sound begin to tug at the
semiconscious mind.
Reluctant to return from this reverie the languid soul slowly stirs.
Completely sated, it longs to linger in this haven of peace
and tranquillity,
But graciously accepts that for now at least it must leave this place.

Megan Fitz-Patrick

YES . . . I'M IN LOVE

Soft touches on skin like snowflakes falling on leaves
The affectionate embrace of hands cupping my face
The light in your eyes as bright as the sun
Yes . . . I'm in love.

A shower of kisses caring and gentle
The long tender holding of me against you
Your smile so warm it melts me
Yes . . . I'm in love.

Our laughter as sweet as birdsong
Shared moments as precious as gold
Fingers linking together in harmony
Yes . . . I'm in love.

Rosalyn Sandercock

BELSEN'S TEARS

(For Dad, Harold Frowen)

I fought in the Second World War
like so many before
and though many horrors I saw
nothing compared to that witnessed at Hell's door
where death's heavy odour hung in the air
like a blanket over the thousands of bodies piled high there
and how my heart wept
for those who now slept
and what they must have endured
before the earth ran red
with the blood that spilled into the soil
but no more will they have to toil
or dance to the tune of pain
as they are finally at peace and rest
for no longer are they Belsen's guests
and yet beyond belief some skeletal souls survived
their strength they revived
by chewing on blades of grass
hoping their hunger would pass
and as I saw them my silent tears fell
whilst the rage inside me began to swell
knowing Man had willingly committed this Holocaust
with no regret for the lives lost
and as I bow my head on Remembrance morn
in tribute of the memory of those who gave their lives
and for those who survived and
as the last post sounds
I know at last their peace
And mine has been found.

Jan Maissen

SOLITUDE

There are no words to express
How my solitude weighs me down
Like an invisible tide
That covers all it touches
It drags me under
And lets me linger there
It embraces me with waves of emotion
And overwhelms me with its sea of unreason
I search for some meaning
But they are only words
And they cannot help me to swim
No reason you can give me
Would explain enough.

Tracy McFarlane

WORDS AND VERSES

To write a poem, I like to take part,
A special poem from the heart.
All my words are meaningful and true,
Especially when they're meant for you.
A poem of nature, a poem of love,
A spiritual poem, like Heaven above.
A poem of sadness, a poem of joy,
A poem for everyone to enjoy.
The poems I write, always rhyme,
Poems in verse all of the time.
Writing poetry means a lot to me,
It relaxes the mind, and makes me free.
Poetry to me is inspiration,
Another way of communication.

Catherine Fleming

REST

There he lay, the old man,
Supine of body, his fragile mind
Struggling wearily to remember
Where he was. Or yet, who he was.
He felt, he realised, very tired
But mistily remembered too,
There had been a time
He had not felt this way;
Dimly recalling that then
His body obeyed his every call.
Dimly recalling, too, that once he had been happy.
He fought with what meagre mental strength he could command
To remember just when that might have been
And what had made it so.
Slowly, so very slowly, the revelation came.
Ah yes. It was when he had been with Caroline.
His beloved Caroline.
He whispered her dear name,
A smile shaping his lips as in his mind's eye
He saw her once again.
He yearned - oh how he yearned -
For that time to come once more.
And miraculously, as he did, she came towards him
Through the mists that gathered in the room.
She smiled at him and said his name
And told him that she loved him,
Gently brushed with her sweet lips
The smile still sat on his
And held his hand
And stroked his brow
And said she'd never leave him.
Then swiftly came there two more visitors -
Those brothers, Sleep and Death.
Sleep came first, with gentle stealth,
Tiring yet more his lids,
Smoothing his visage, quietening his breath.
Then stole in Death
Who, judging now the time was ripe,

Joined hands with his brother Sleep,
To give the old man their precious gift
Of everlasting Rest.
And peace.

G F Pash

THE FESTIVAL OF DAWN

The still sound of silence that trembles in the air,
A single bell, a dog that barks,
A distant cockerel crowing,
Gradually the orchestra of morning slowly growing.
The festival of dawn begun,
The thrusting rush of rising sun,
The fierce and fiery glow transforms
The sky with liquid light.
The world begins to breathe anew
And wakens from the night.
But still the waiting silence deep
As shrouded houses silent sleep,
Then a single sound would quiver,
Sending up wild geese that shiver
Into fiery dawn,
Chorusing another morn.
A single star through rain-washed grey
Gives welcome to another day.
Again the urgent cockerel crows
And children huddle under bedclothes
And babies cry and lovers sigh.
The silence simply melts away,
And night capitulates to day.

Kristin MacEwan

DANCEHALL MEDITATIONS

I see
A sea
Of coloured faces
On dancing strangers -
As spectral starburst streams
Flow like liquid
Across my visual.
It did seem unusual
To be in a room
That moved
In unison
To one song -
The beat of someone's
One drum
And bass -
That keeps pace with
Hearts racing,
Butts shaking,
Feet pacing
To the music -
Hard enough to leave the floor with bruises,
Yet fast enough for our minds to use it
In communicating subliminal truths which
Connect us
Even better than sex does,
Almost like love -
As if this could solve
All the world's
Problems at once.
So let's try
And unite
All of them,
Under these tunes -
Hands raised
In high fives
And mock military salutes.
Make use
Of the lips
God gave you
To kiss,
Knock back drinks,

Sing to the bits
Of the lyrics
You knew -
Not abuse:
But just come together like atoms become molecules -
'Cause when we split
We release a fire
Brighter
Than any fuel -
That consumes
The world
In mushroom curls -
Swallowing men, women, boys and girls.
'Cause young and old can live mayfly lives -
When taken in the blink of an eye
By explosive suicidal solutions.
Sky TV shows us how families die
With all their children -
And, we realise,
That the only race
Disgraced
By genocide
Is human.
So I'd rather choose this
Musical movement -
It's beautiful
Simply to
Move to the music.
These moments
Don't need you to sacrifice or take lives
Just do it.
The only price
Is that you celebrate life -
As you live through it.

Tomas Adejumo

TURNING POINT

And so the longest day of the year sped by
Lifted on the smiling backs of gulls
And tugged by on the breeze that graced us
There on our hill, watching the sky wheel overhead.

My flesh still warms to that sun's caress
On your skin.
My smile still remembers your hand -
Heavy with the softness of you.

There was a kite,
And the crash of surf below us.
There were distant shouts,
And the brief, wet nose of a questing dog.
There were the scents of crushed grass
And your hair - spun glass on the breeze
Reaching out.

I'll swear we passed a lifetime there,
In that echoing day that rushed past us,
Taken on the tide of words spoken
And words silent.
And I'll swear at the last your dandelion breath
Puffed the summer stars into the sky,
Hushing with the dying of the day.

The force that pricked them through it
Pushed me to my back,
Where the earth gently gifted me the day's heat
And I, awed, wept for it all -
Two tiny tears I passed off as hayfever.

We left before the night grew cold.
And you believed me.

The bedrock of my soul
Still gives back that day's heat,
I only have to close my eyes
And I'm blinded again by midsummer sunlight,
Lost in the place of the new colours
Seen obliquely by the sun through your eyes.

I cannot remember one word of that day.
Not even your name.
And so its treasure lives on secure;
High on its everlasting hillside.

Fay Roberts

A CHORUS TIME

In the inky darkness
Of deep sapphire hue
A single bird breaks into
The night-time stillness.
This lone voice begins
A sparkling song
And
Before very long
Silhouettes on aerials
Shady shapes in trees
Join the avian choir -
Each tune its own
But
Not cacophony, pure
Symphony.

The sky lightens -
Starting in the east
Pale pinky-apricot fingers
Grasp the horizon
Heralding the rising sun -

While reluctantly the sleepers,
Prodded into consciousness,
Lurch forward
Into the brand new day.

Geri Laker

WORRIES

I'm beside myself with worry,
Which worries me,
Because if I'm beside myself,
Where does this leave myself?
If the only context to my being
Is in my being worried
Then I find myself worrying;
Where would I be without it?

Indeed, I've been overcome
By the worry won
From failure to keep it at bay.
But what would happen if it went away?
A man without worry
Is a man without problems
And a man without problems should worry,
For, to worry is to be concerned.

The problem as far as I'm concerned
Is that I worry too much
About whether my concerns are a problem
And whether this problem should concern me.
It concerns me that if it didn't
That would be a worry,
For if my problems couldn't concern me,
Who could they concern?
Do you see my problem?

And yet, despite all this worry,
My problem concerning the extent of my worry
Remains the same.
If I'm beside myself as not myself,
Am I myself and not beside myself,
Or myself beside myself
Just worrying about nothing?
Oh, if only that were true!

If that were true
And I'm worrying about nothing,
Then that would make myself nothing
And the self beside myself nothing
And I'd be worrying about becoming nothing,
Twice!
Which is a problem of quite concern.

I'm worried.

Robert Casey

THE WEDDING TREE

Its shadow lay long over the lawn
before it was reduced in height.
Now it looks more motherly wide.
Three spikes form an aspiring crown,
from where the birds sing at dawn.

A cat peers up at the desirable sight.
Then it goes into comfort pose
and sits, ears twitching,
faking rest, it purrs
as if resigned to its plight.

The fir is a perfect hiding place
for jubilant loving in spring.
The crown now has three spires
from where the lovers sing
a twitter blues into blue space.

In this green steepled castle
tweet weddings are sanctified
and under cat-proof roofs
bird love is multiplied.
All sing the rite of spring at eventide.

Helga Hopkinson

BRIGHT EMBERS

It pats,
Like rain yet thick, impure, tainted.
Round splatters as it hits, smacks,
Against a cold ground,

They flow,
An endless stream of liquid sorrow,
As it pats,
Pats, an echo in the dark,
Running free, stretching, staining,

A dirty, slimy thing,
Crawling woefully in the dark,
Blind, its eyes area closed,
As it pulls itself along,

Wrapping and tying,
Distressingly alone,
It hides, in its silver blanket,
Curling as a teardrop,

A moth or a butterfly?
Can it stretch its wings?
As it pulls from the cocoon,
Bright wings of fluttering beauty,

Darkness retreating, the colours break free,
Bright embers of pure wondrous light,
Like glistening dazzles of a crown
As it crawls in the crimson,

Flickering out splatters gently,
As it gracefully spreads
Its large wings and cascades
Into the burning light.

Scarlett York

PLACE OF DREAMS

I can't afford to get to know you again
To unlock the reservoir of emotion
That for so long has been dammed
By a false and destructive façade
To set out on a journey
You openly acknowledge
Might not have a destination
How can I possibly consider such foolhardy action?
What would possess me to do it?
Emptiness
Longing
To once more connect
And be taken to that place of dreams
Where thought and feeling overwhelm
And love engulfs you
To the point of ecstasy.

Marion Blake

REGRETS

Oh this torment within my heart
The stifled screams that echo
Endlessly throughout the labyrinths
Of my mind.
Misted eyes that barely hide
The pain of grief,
Arms that long to hold,
Hands to touch.
She who is no longer there,
Those words I did not speak,
The nightmares of my soul.

Austin Baines-Brook

BELGIUM 2007

That first meeting -
Me, presuming you were just another blond himbo
But you surprised me no end
And proved that first impressions are ominous

The restaurant . . . speaking Italian,
Your humour and intelligence - my wit and wisecracks
The 'American Chicken' and the constant banter and laughter

Sitting at the bar later you told me you felt a real connection
(Nothing to do with the copious amount of wine we'd drunk then?)
But that I had an aura about me - Funny? I felt that with you too
Couldn't explain it, couldn't put my finger on why, or how
But it was . . . Nice.

The ball . . . the builders . . . the laughs
Escaping the mad crowds and drunk men to dance to our own tune
'You dance nice,' you told me. 'Ditto,' I replied
And again the rhythm and connection struck a chord

We continued the rest of the weekend in much the same vein
Drinking, laughing, feeling closeness
That normally takes years to build on
A past life? A future friendship? Who knows? Who cares

But something clicked that crazy on-off weekend in Belgium
We were meant to meet - for whatever rhyme or reason
And no matter what, it'll always stay with me -
Be it just a fond memory or anything else
Hope it does for you too.

Sal Barker

TO THE SEA

We love you;
when lazily teasing,
ebbing and flowing,
with a lover's kisses
you caress the shore.

We love you,
when reflecting the blue
of a cloudless sky.
Or when on fire with the setting sun,
or when silvery mysterious
with the moon at full
on a summer night
when day is done.

We fear you
when hissing and slapping,
your thunder roars,
seething and pounding
against the rocks.

We fear you
splashing and crashing
with mountainous strength
eternally with us,
before and hereafter,
angrily churning in cavernous depths.
Oh! Wondrous, living, mighty water,
we love and we fear you.

Lydia Storey

TREE OF LIFE

Forbidden fruit, Thou shalt not eat,
Guarded by angels, inaccessible,
Thought to be in Iraq, where the
Tigris and Euphrates meet.

Some think they've identified the tree -
Old, shrivelled, nothing on it;
More like a dead tree in Winter
Than the lush centrepiece of the Garden of Eden.

Then, someone at church showed us a picture,
Asian, it shows the Tree of Life
In all its glory - with Christ crucified,
And now I get it!

The old Tree of Life - beautiful, alive,
Forbidden, defiled;
The new Tree of Life - gory, ugly, dead,
Now accessible, healing, bringing Life to
Anyone who wants it -
Come, taste and see that it is good.

Kathy Rawstron

TEARS

The tears sting, as I wish things were different,
The tears burn, as I know it's too late,
The tears fall, as I see you with her.
The blade cuts, an answer to my problems,
The blade slices, a reminder of my mistakes,
The blade slashes, an outlet for my pain.
The blood seeps, stopping all thought,
The blood spills, overpowering all feeling,
The blood flows, flooding all emotion.
The tears stop.

Zoe Bailey

WHITE STALLION

Along the stretch of deserted beach,
Pounding hooves on virgin sands.
The whispering shush of moving sea.
White stallion splashes in bubbling surf
Playfully riding the waves.

Gently grazing, lips caressing
Nibbling tenderly on wild tufted grasses,
White stallion lingers on.

A bird catches his twinkling eye
White stallion bolts -
An explosion of speed,
Determinedly racing,
Feels like flying.

Stallion's hooves stroke
The untouched desert's skin.
The earth trembles
In anticipation.

Rhythmically galloping
On strong muscular haunches.
Pulsating and throbbing.
Wind blowing through silky pure mane.

Heart beating rapidly,
Heavy breathing, nostrils flared.
A bullet speeding like wild fire.
White stallion rears and
Cries out in pleasure.

Across the amber dunes
Into the setting sun
White stallion gracefully walks
A solitary path of happiness.

Wendy Sharp

A WAITING MIRROR

Around the myriad essence of the face,
The soft creases and bright effusions
Delicate sent forth,
Is the wry yet playful frown
I smile upon the most.
As river's ripples disrupt the well-known surface,
Delight is in the known disruption,
As the same recurrent pictures
Play again in thought.
As the inconstant images
Of the still or undulating water
Constant in the mind remain
Known visions, unthreatening to thought,
The image of rippling and the unseen deeper waves
More delightful still are made
By the floating petals,
Stucco of stalks and flowers,
Draped into the waters,
As some sweet recurrence of the bejewelled waves
Seems to swell the wondrous scene,
At once silent and serene,
To some intransient ideal,
Left forever self-imbued and with the mind entwined.
And so, the mild frown,
The furrowed brows which crown
The indrawn cheeks and piled lips
When it returns is so,
And seems to show,
Recurrent beauty stays the mind
From outside itself
Its meaning there to find.
But now, from the furrowed surface
With flowers once endowed,
The revolving march
And floating army of the times
Parades itself, with a spread of half-drowned packets.
The disregarded papers
And worn tools of every day present
The arboreous ardours of a life
That spreads itself
So thin about the Earth.

Thin but great to stain
Each surface left,
Uncovered by itself.
The rueful watching of the eye
Perceives with gloom all the way before it.
The petals paired with waste as well as flowers
As the hand of Millais strews
Plastics in the golden locks
That drew his lover down.
And as the surface ripples with its waste,
Heavy dark and brown,
The calm recumbent petal's beauty
Seems to bring a burden,
Urging towards return.
As when the face serene
Becomes blistered with a fury
Or in floods of tears is drowned,
The burden reappears.
As the hands reclaim the water's surface
And the Earth's beauty is made free
And clean of Man's foul makings;
I have smoothed the now calm surface
That I may perceive mine serene.

Nathaniel Payne

TIME

It slips past without a whisper
Each moment a moment gone
Memories, memories fade
In the twilight
A light may flicker
But in the blink of an eye
You will be gone
And time will slip past
             to find another

Harry Thomson

THE WHINBUSHES

(So often we look in all the wrong places and to the wrong people, expecting to find there the great things the soul longs for - like love, hope, wisdom, truth, or to grasp a hold on some mystery. But just like we always have to learn, that it is in humbler places or from the least of people that we find those things. So it was with this poem, which was inspired by the meanest and most common of all nature's children, the whinbush when she is out in her yellow flower each Easter. Dedicated to all those who have suffered in Ireland during the troubles and to all those who have suffered in our world.)

What is this now upon the whins?
From where came such deep beauty which crowns their heads?
That lay colourless throughout winter's night
When giving shelter to bare beast and shadeless sheep
Protecting from sleet's teeth and iron jaws.
Why now when before I saw nothing in their common green?
Yet what beauty lay within when invisible?
The mystery bright lay through the yellow coloured sun,
Splashed on, head upon head.
Awaking from sleep on grove and all free ground,
Mountain tops and hills where no furrow was ever turned
And upon fences leaning the same as within deep friendship,
Now with these things I go, as they take me through to the sacred places
Where my soul can ask for the answers to close the span.
From where and when or how it came to be, that glory rests on such.
Then came the whisper it was by me and my creative hand,
And time's first words spoke unto her seed,
With this I cherished what before was unknown to me
And fondling dear with thought wondered to what I can give these things.
To stand as guard and defence against time, change or forgetfulness.
She spoke this time and I knew it was her first and last.
So I listened with the whole Earth and all Man's ears.
She said, 'Give me to the hurt and weak, to those done wrong,
Sufferers of injustice, fear, hatred, ignorance and gain.
And overall, in earth or sky or sea give me to thousands
Slain and maimed by pain.
And through us when our flower each year you see
Remember! Remember! Never forget what we had.
And if we don't choose peace then what we'll have instead
Of our yellow coloured sun will turn to blood.'

Samuel Irwin

DEMOLITION OF GRANDMA'S HOUSE

You are not there in reality,
But logic vies with heart and soul,
A part of whom still live there.
Demolition, the rising of new bricks,
Rape of childhood cherished place.
Memory compensates anguish.

Smell of deep-shine wooden things,
Stained-glass windows, scullery stove.
Long red rugs on lino floors,
Window seats over cubby-holes.
Echoing click of sitting-room door,
Ancient hoover, traffic drone.

Sixteen stairs - eight in twos,
Shallow hand-basin, cracked for years.
Small cosy room with hard, high bed,
Casement windows on ropes that stuck.
Lulled to sleep by night city lights.
Holiday dreams of being grown up.

More than mere walls, inanimate friend,
I, soaked in your atmosphere
Took refuge in hospitality.
Twenty-five years I knew your ways,
Creaks and cracks, moods and schemes,
And you knew me, Number Twenty-Three.

Liz Parker

ROUTE 27

A sea of foam breezing in the heavens,
looking down on speeding mediums
coercing their way on grey asphalt lines,
leading to final aspirations.

Static hedge, with lime foliage shudders,
trees flutter new limbs, like feathers
fly, on exhilarating breath of Thor,
as he sweeps black vapour in his path.

Mesmerising white broken lines race by,
yard by yard, blurring into one,
one yard stretching until distant trail ends.
Single droplets splatter on the screen.

A sea of foam breezing in the heavens,
looking down on speeding mediums.

Rita Pedrick

MARC

(1980 - 2003)

There is an empty space
Which you once filled
With joy, laughter and happiness,
But your young life was cut short
And now you lie in endless sleep,
Surrounded by love and tranquillity.
I think of you all the time,
At home, at work and in my sleep,
The pain, the sorrow and the grief
Never leaves, it's always there.
Your beautiful face, your cheeky smile,
Your gentle voice, your loving ways,
Are all stored inside my head and my heart,
With all your treasured memories,
Now, forever and always.

Kevin Huntley

THE WAY WE LEAD FOR OTHERS

The souls of those whom lived before
Are what we are today.
The love (or hate) they kept in store
Is left for us to play.
A little dance in summer's sun,
To run along the shore;
Or drag the carcass hate has clung
And left to rot in store.

The halo of sweet innocence
To shield the little child.
The guiding hand to teenage pain,
Help stop them turning wild.
A listening ear to troubles share
So they are not alone,
May help prevent much violence flare
And hearts that turn to stone.

Pearl M Burdock

THE OLD APPLE ORCHARD

All winter in the threadbare orchard
tipsy trees leaned drunken here and there.
Some, losing rootage to defeating winds,
lay almost prone; limbs frail or broken.

But now in spring, their thin sap rises
and like ageing, bent, arthritic ladies
trying on the faded, pale pink ball dress
they'd waltzed in years ago,
the old trees bedeck their boughs
in sparse-sprinkled blossom,
faint echoes of their past profusion
and bloom of fruitful youth.

Elizabeth Clarke

YESTERDAY AND BEYOND

Behind the time which
Races across my spectrum now,
Lies tomorrow and the day after and beyond,

Yesterday has gone, been committed to my memory,
Of which I will always be extremely fond,
But the future has to be my anthem, my song.

Hope is the chariot I ride through the night,
Never to be eclipsed on the shores of oblivion in the early morning light,
Smiles and expectations are strapped on tomorrow's mast,
Tears and recriminations lie tethered with yesterday's past,

While the bright hue of anticipation gleams out on my horizon,
I head to my future with my generation, my peers,
To right the wrongs, forging a fresh new order,
A place where every man, woman and child have their space,
Where the new order's anthem everybody knows and hears.

Gone and locked on yesterday's dark side are those who stood tall
Brothers on the shoulders of their lesser brother to pocket the proceeds
Of the pain and gain dispensed at their orders, at their command,
Issued at will to an innocent brotherhood of men.

So behind the time which
Trips cross my spectrum now,
Lies tomorrow and the day after and beyond,
For yesterday has gone and lies bleeding in a quiet corner of my mind,
But some of yesterday forever I will be fond,
Now only the future and tomorrow can be my anthem, my song,
Because tomorrow will soon be yesterday and beyond.

P J Littlefield

BRAVE NU WURLLED

In the fewcher thair will be
no torcher, miserrie, spyte or spellin,
wich involes all three.
You think I'm jokeing?
Think of tirranie and failyure,
think of scorn and clever cloggs' kontemppt
for thowse of us that canot tell
funetics from our funny bone.
The constant teese
of i's and e's
and wich wai rownd they goe,
and all thowse meen old letters
wich do absollewtley nothing -
as in knobblie nees and nitting
nats and gnomes.
Yu do not punish thwose in weelchairs.
It's no shayme to wair glases.
Shakespeer rote his name
five difrent wais
and no wun larfs at him.
I noe my Bibul.
Reed Sarm ten, vurse tow,
and if yu can reed this
then wot's the point of spellin?

Margaret Franks

INCONSEQUENTIAL NOTHINGS

Let us talk of nothing in particular,
Of early morning cups of tea,
And socks warming on the radiator.
The favourite song playing on the radio
As you sip the creamy froth from your hot chocolate,
The lyrics forming too easily on your lips.
Let us talk of lazy Sunday mornings
And even lazier afternoons.
Soft sprung spring grass underfoot
And dappled sunlight on your skin.
At one end of the year, the crunch of autumn leaves,
And at the other, the cool caress of a summer breeze.
Let us mention fireworks,
Their too bright colours exploding overhead
And dazzling eyes.
Let us not forget the salty sea air,
The crash of waves upon a golden shore.
While the sea air whips through your hair,
Let us speak of rosy sunsets,
Dramatic colours contrast darkest silhouettes
As reds and yellows fade to midnight blues
And all the stars wink into existence.
Let us mention freshly baked bread
And the smell of peppermints,
And vanilla, rose and lavender.
Perhaps we should even speak of laughter,
The tearful eyes and sore stomachs caused by excess,
And the joy of a room full of giggles and sniggers and chuckles.
Let us think of dearest friends,
Those who know us far too well,
Those with whom we gossip, chat and cry,
All shared over a cup of coffee
And a biscuit or two. (Or even three!)
Let us talk of brief shared glances,
The secret smiles, the pinkness in the cheeks.
Maybe even the feel of a lover's hand in yours
As you walk along the street.

Let us talk indeed of all these things
And then tell me
That they are nothing, nothing at all, but
Inconsequential.

Glynnis Morgan

SMILOLOGY

Dare
Dare to do it:
Raise your lips and
Form a smile.

People
May well wonder
At the reason:
It can beguile.

Smiling's
So contagious
You can't help
But emulate.

Joy
So substantial
A mere smile
Can relate.

Pleasure
Needs expression:
Effusive
Smilology.

So dare
Dare to do it:
Raise your lips, and
Smile for me!

Belinda Ludlow

A PLAYER IN THE THEATRE OF DREAMS

I settled down upon my lawn
Replete with bread and wine,
It's a perfect middle, in a perfect day.
The house and grounds around me, models of perfection,
A horse is grazing in a field nearby.
'Twixt the sound of babbling brook
And a blackbird on a branch,
Comes the laughter of my children from the garden.

As I wander back towards the house,
I see my darling wife,
Resplendent in her gown of purest white.
Could any man, I ask myself, desire much more from life
Than all of which I can see laid out before me?
I wander through each room,
Every corridor and staircase,
I touch each painting, carpet, wall and statue.

I am woken from my sleep
By a screaming 'lager lout'.
I reach out my hand and touch my cardboard walls;
For the mansion I am in
Has paper carpets, oh! so thin,
I can feel the cold
Invading every bone.

Next time you see a down 'n' out
So apparently sad 'n' scruffy,
Remember, he too aspires to greater things;
But he confines his aspirations
To the mansion of his dreams,
And thanks God for sleep
To see the other side.

Kay Reynolds

TEARS OF A FLOATING SPIRIT (A SOLDIER'S DEATH)

He walks with the reviving impressions constantly on his mind,
Of his friends so dear lost within a war of no reason,
No sympathy and no excuses.
Tormented by his loss he treads the dark vast spaces.
His thoughts only of his comrades he left behind,
Their bloodstained faces infest his mind.

Yet as he drifts, he's oblivious to the fact that it's he
Who floats the sky, not his friends.
His spirit not accepting that its body is dead
And that he was lost within that war of hollow victories.
Finally he realises 'twas them that survived,
Stabs at him time and again, like the bayonet in his side.

In time he'll find that the dead mourn more for the living,
His ghost is morbid where his faith was once strong.
His spirit crushed - his demise infinite.
His destruction meant the escape of excruciating pain, but not woe
And as poppies are sold by the ton,
Spirits weep constantly like bullets from a gun.

Kelvin Smith

LAKELAND WINGS

The air emblazoned with the urge of attack
And led us half-wrapped in unfinished argument
Amongst rock lost brigantines
The intolerable salt rage and harsh beauty
When the perfume of the roses stopped
Across pattern grown lovely whorled pasture
Flying seashells form blossom on white horse hill
So long as flower patterns
Capture our memory
As the eagle and the dove
Co-supreme in nature's star pageants.

Edward Tanguy

VIRTUALLY

Poised above your smile
Like sunshine on ice
My dearest avatar
I'm your bunch of pixels
Our prescribed distances equidistant
to my snap yap chasing its tail
I long to have you tactile
and not frozen at your dazzling teleport
for next mission
Bugs that bite in the shadows of the
light illuminating the all of our nothingness
The intent of our 'minds' grappling with dead thoughts
wept up like sour lives blazing trajectories
Interlocking only when the trail fades
and I'm struck lonely in the mwahs and lols
of capsized 'reality'.

Olivia McCarthy

AUTUMNAL GLORY

Marvelling at the autumnal glory of nature,
Trees and bushes with their riot of colour
Even though they are not the myriad
Hues of summer
Rather the yellow, brown
And burnt orange of the evening
Of the year.
Long gone are the bright hot days
Summer has merged into autumn
Soon, the autumn leaves would fall
And be tossed in the wind
Then wither, die and be swept out
Of sight, just as her love would
Be swept away in the bustle
And bustle of everyday life.

Joana Sam-Avor

THE HAUNTING OF POET BY SNAIL

Has it been four days now?
Must have been . . . nearly a week . . .
since I did the deed. It was dark,
and I was hurrying; I didn't see
his form, the path in front of me.
My careless size ten shoe came down
and crushed his hopes and dreams.

My stride stopped mid-step. Sickened
by that sound, the chilling crunch;
I saw him, when I lifted up.
A tragic mix of slime and shrapnel.

And now, although you'll doubt,
I swear he's back. I am the mollusc's
sole unfinished business
on this fast and brutal Earth.

You'll say it's in my head, if report
that I can hear his death
in every mistimed gearshift,
every mouth devouring crisps.

But it's not my conscience doing this,
it's him. He's putting me through Hell.
I hear, with every step I take,
the breaking of the tell-tale shell.

Last night I thought I saw him,
bright and cold, in death.
Slowly sliding next to me,
and felt his tiny, ghostly breath.

'It was dark!' I scream. 'I was hurrying!'
His silence says it all. But still,
you don't believe me? Come on round,
see the trails across my walls . . .

and explain the vengeful holes
in my fridge-ridden, cellophaned lettuce.

Jamie McGarry

MATTHEW'S DEATH

A groschen, Matthew, brought you death,
a silly old sou was your theft,
an act intended to nourish your kids;
    your children
      suffering in dearth.

Clean of heart but for this one misdeed:
Family love the seed of your crime;
But in time you were brought to the dock,
    Matthew,
      from Medernach.

The judge's decision was heartless
- a noble of ignoble art -
your execution on Hanging Hill
    witnessed
      by wife and kin.

L J Feeney

WHY WALK PAST MY HOUSE?

My eyes had grown accustomed to the sight
but even so my heart still winced each time
forgiveness has abandoned me tonight.
I watch as their hands swing a rhythmed chime
of love, like youngsters showing off their pact.
Clasped hands together swinging out a beat
it makes me sick to watch this spurious act
my mind's made up, his sentence now complete.
The man who once lay promised in my bed.
The man who took his see-through love from me.
The man who snarled at me to 'Drop down dead'
who jibed his faithfulness would never be.
That man's now lifeless, bloodstains spoil her coat
his screams of *'No'* stuck ever in his throat.

Kathryn Swainson

SHADOWS

Shimmering ripples on a foaming sea,
Elusive wisps to a grasping hand.
Stark black images on burning sand.
Graffiti.

Gentle portraits on the lawn
Sometimes play upon the grass.
Dancers pulled together,
No respecter of time,
A partner from today, another from yesteryear
Adult, reborn as a child within the play.

Artefacts, dredged from ancient history,
Tango with the travails of yesterday
As the wind plays with the cast of forest leaves.
Fearsome creatures chasing a frightened man,
Galloping like ghosts.

Products of the night, lost in the light.
These are the shadows of the mind.

William Harris

DISCLOSURE

Tonight is a balloon
in the hands of a magician.

It could be many things.
A flower. A giraffe. A bow tie. A dog.

From there the city lights look like bubbles,
swelling in the velvet sky.

There's always a moment,
when a can starts to hiss,
that you begin to see the foreseeable.

Somewhere in the city
                you're asleep with him.

Ben Ashwell

THE ANGER POOL

I walk down a dusted path,
Newly lined with skeleton trees
And lightly trimmed with snow
At the top of my mind is clear
My breathing steady
But as each step descends
My thoughts cascade
Like the torrent of a waterfall
To break upon the rocks
And bruise me with repetition.

And there it is, waiting for me
Like a pool I can't avoid
I must step into its darkness
And be swallowed by its bitterness
The deeper I proceed
The sharper my thoughts become
Until they too are bitter
And gleam with icy barbs
To tear at my indifference
And line my words with bile.

From somewhere the bubble of a thought erupts
And holds lazily above my eyes
Carelessly idle and ill-formed
I watch with hope that it might rise
And burst upon the surface
A beacon to a passer-by
But despite coaxing it remains
With words emblazoned across its belly
Suggesting that my usefulness
Is a mirror to its pointlessness.

I wonder if my presence is enough
To displace the level of this pool
If I have produced enough of anything
To form the tiniest of waves
To splash upon either shore
And leave a slickened line
That might signify to others
That something other than themselves
Has mind enough to matter
And matters enough to make a difference.

But from here I cannot see
Neither sun nor starry sky
And the memories of which are growing cold
From here all that I can see
Is the darkness to which I stride
And all that I hear is a pounding heart
And words I take for someone else's
Telling me that where I'm going
Only takes the couched and clotted
And has opened its arms to me.

It swallows me, this pool
It takes away my room to breathe
And feeds me its fermented anger
And strips my of myself
It holds me, this darkness
Until the point is gone to see
And the will to try has vanished
Only the shell remains to echo
The propaganda that has bleached my skin
And left anger where I used to be.

Choiceless I move on
A little deeper, a little slower
A little angrier with every step
With the knowledge that persists
Of an end to this beginning
And if I were to stop and turn around
I would be lost without a doubt
So I move on regardless
With the buoyancy of a stone
To a goal I once had a mind to regard.

In the epicentre of my traverse
I am startled by a chorus
That rise up from silt and stench
To honour guard my passage
A triptet of guttural wails
That pierce me through and through
And eye me with expectation
As if I might with slight persuasion
Flap tongue at the occasion
Of my joining their crew.

Repulsion makes a puppet of my walk
And has me swinging with Nguyen's rhythm in the noose
Blood burrows deep and seeks to escape
But finds no fissure to facilitate
Leaving an empty-headed rattle in reply
I close my eyes begging darkness to return
To hide the repugnant chorus from view
But etched within my eyelids
Is their ghostly silhouette
And their wails mine my mind for sanity.

The shadow of his corpse
Raised welts upon their skin
To which they were oblivious
Too enamoured were they
With their own prognostications
That I too would be slapping ruddy gums
And beating hollow causes
And contentedly plucking at the words
That absently fell from porous mouths
And shaping them into rusted quips.

In gestures of camaraderie
That inflicts me like blight
They part to let me pass
And I shuffle on my harrowed way
They close ranks and puff with pride
To accomplishments they never made
And bore holes into my twisted spine
That writhes like a keelback
And threatens to leave me limp
And at the mercy of every passing whim.

Then out of the gloom she appeared
On a lean and long ago neglected
Carved in a fixed convivial expression
Cloaked in continual tiny waves of green
Thinking that I'd found reprieve
I placed my cheek against the coldness of her pedestal
And looked up into her distant gaze with admiration
Wanting more than merely to be wanting
Needing more than granite would allow
Asking less and dissolving my expectations.

I shiver and try to outlast the ice
That grows around my limbs
But my shaking disrupts the rubble
And causes her to lean a little more
And with that self-same smile she lets me known
That my time has already come
And in an instant the ice has set me free
I peel away my cheek and move to stand
Her gesture hasn't changed but leaves me in no doubt
That were she to speak I'd be standing too close for comfort.

I am the punctured bellows at the forge
I am the fragments that fly from the chisel
The rag that's used to wipe away the bleeding wound
Of a hero in some mythic battle depicted on canvas
The shattered quill too brittle to be of use
The thoughts that never make it to the page
I am the dust that falls upon the loom
Within the walls that crack and start to fall
That's swept aside when waters start to rise
And was lost before the house was long forgotten.

I stumble and I fall and try to rise
I feed upon the bitterness that ruptures from inside
I fix my eyes on a slight discolouration
And head in that direction though I've long forgotten why
Thoughts flutter like a draught and can't be captured
Feelings form but are very quickly mixed
Until they lose all self and feel the same
And are used to feed the knot that's at my core
The knot by which I'm now identified.

My feet find a slope and I emerge
Soaked to the marrow and completely redefined
Burning in the absence of my passions
Furrowed in the absence of my thoughts
Slickened by the rivulets cascading down my spine
Hollowed without the desire to be satiated
I take my steps and silently deliver
Breaths upon the wind that quickly disappear
Words to ears without the will to listen
Heartbeats to a rhythm no one else will hear.

Craig McGeady

WET DEATH

The cold;
A strange thing, especially if it's in the form of water;
Something which we have plenty of, but we also lack.

Ever felt the cold run down your body like a deadly waterfall?
Ever felt your body totally submerged in wet death?

Either way, I have.

Being totally covered in cold liquid, it makes me feel safe.
It makes me feel like no harm can come to me, that I'm
                                        covered in armour
Although I am just a few centimetres from the surface.
But it also makes me feel vulnerable lying there in the open.

It makes me feel strong knowing that I can cope
With the cold and what death it can bring.
Knowing that it is wrapping deadly vines around my merciful body.

My body breathes the water and not the air.
The water is pure and clean, but the air is stuffy and carries evil souls.

The water kills in many ways,
Either by not being there, or too much of it in one place.
Death follows it wherever it flows.
We can't escape it, it's nature.

There are many myths about the sea,
But the true one is that it's made of souls.
The flowing of it is them moving,
The wetness is them weeping,
Weeping for forgiveness,
For loneliness,
Or even happiness.

Water;
We take so much from it,
But it always takes so much from us.
The love we have for it is so strong that it draws us to it.
We praise it. We would die for it. We live for it.

The whole water of our bodies,
The graveyard of our fellow race,
The one thing which divides us from them,
The one thing that keeps us sleeping.

Without it, we would not be here.

But without it, I would not be who I am.
And for me to share my love for the sea
Is the only love I have ever had,
And the one thing which makes me feel strong.

The one thing which makes me pure.

Emma Croshaw

ON WATCHING A PROGRAMME ABOUT WORDSWORTH AND BEING DISTINCTLY UNIMPRESSED, MAY 2009

At one point he delivers his monologue
while standing on the wrong bridge
and I feel slightly bemused.
Seeing a place on TV that I've been
yet feeling no connection to it.
Which is odd.
Such is the way of London.

Soap opera elements of W's life
are interesting to a point but
biographical conjecture is
presented as fact
and I feel mildly bothered.
Such is the way of TV.

My attention is not held and
my mind wanders to you.
It is an easy leap from Westminster Bridge
but I know that showing you this
would be misconstrued.
Such is the way of people.

Richard Gough Thomas

RATHMULLAN SHORE STROLL

What is the destiny
Of seashells on the shore?

Having held invertebrates
Now cast on beaches
Like hard trained vanguards
Of an invading force
Whose bombers failed to deliver
Enough accurate payloads
To provide cover
As at Omaha last century

Or . . .

Are they fleeing crabs
And seabirds seeking sustenance?

Or . . .

To lie there
Catching unsuspecting bare feet?

But bringing them home
In sandy pockets
Holds a memory
Of strolling silent
With gambolling dogs
Windswept and tousled
Peace, perfection, Rathmullan.

P Murphy

PROUD

Sometimes tears just roll down my sharp cheeks
As feelings for them cascade within my being
Exploding with the enormity of these two people
Who are so central in my life, so proud am I
A smile, quite broad, creeps cross my face
Attracting eyes of people in the street
'Strange woman crying, smiling broadly all at once,' their faces say
They can't see my bursting, love-filled heart.

Amanda Walker

LOVE'S ILLUSION

With your quirky smile I was well impressed,
A handsome young god who outshone the rest,
Conquest complete on my sixteenth birthday.

On foreign shores we strolled hand in hand,
Sea breezes kissing vainglorious suntans,
As frail sun sprayed gold dust over dying day.

Arrogant as only young lovers could be,
Thinking the world belonged to you and me.
We had it all, what more was there to say.

A golden couple but surprise, surprise,
The illusion collapsed before my eyes.
Death of romance a bitter price to pay.

Shame crawled like maggots across my skin
Demanding confession for an unknown sin.
Dying inside, a wide smile on display.

Electricity that once flowed at a touch
Fizzled into flashes of listless lust,
Stars stopped shining and the moon turned away.

Warm caresses, once familiar, now gone,
Still scent and sensation in dreams live on
Turning my limbs into unmoulded clay.

Breakfasts heralded that thousand-mile stare
Present in body yet mind off elsewhere,
Tumbling down dark hills, unwilling to stay.

So I didn't share, afraid you would run,
Too late anyway, damage already done.
Silence perhaps, might hold Devil at bay.

Parting, a bridge waiting to be crossed,
Death by degrees, yet not all was lost
For fate had left one last card to play.

Life, like Lady Luck, is sometimes a bitch
Dressed up in a tunic of shoddy tricks
Yet she brought joy into my world today.

Fight over, I surrendered, panic gone,
For cradled in my arms is our newborn son.

Kathleen Potter

US OR THEM

Darkness, the parting gift of the waning moon
Soon the dawn will seep its light onto the stage
The actors of this macabre scene line up
Like boys waiting to be chosen for a playground game
Or rather, guilty men, condemned to death
With their backs against the wall, uncertain of their fate
Every morning they stand and wait
To watch and listen for the faintest of signs
The slightest noise made by the harbinger of their doom

Stomachs knotted with bile and nails bitten to the quick
Time passes slowly, every second a lifetime
Every minute more than their shattered nerves can bear
The morning mist veils the truth, a curtain across the future
Sounds are muffled and shadows swirl, taunting lies of imagined forms
They strain to hear, deafened by the rain of shell
Unleashed night and day for days past
The silence now loud in their drumming ear
Senses dulled as by a blanket, smothering and thick

And then they come, like wraiths in grey
Conjured from the colourless haze
Deadly purpose in their every stride, weapons thrust forward
The sharpened points beckon the eye with glistening splendour
And with this sight comes sounds of many not yet seen
Through senses suddenly sharp and focused
Time slows and heartbeat quickens, the taste of fear coats the tongue
As rifles raise and press to shoulder, staring eyes take careful aim
And choose the lives that will end this day

Then hell breaks loose and weapons thunder
Lines of men slump to earth like emptied sacks
Stripped of life, become mere obstacles to the men behind
Stepped over like sleeping dogs, but they'll wake no more
Just rot where they fell and fertilise the land they came to conquer
Still more come, only to fall under the rain of lead and shrapnel
That spurt from heated barrel and screaming shell
Molten steel scythes through their ranks
Clothing, bones, flesh and lives asunder

And now it's done and as the smoke clears
The true horror of the deed seeps into their souls
Men, turned to crazed demons by fear and loathing
Become the simple soldiers they were before
Before this onslaught twisted their minds
Made them slaughter their fellow man
They sit and stare at the enemy's remains
And as the day turns to dusk, beg God for forgiveness
With a bloodied sleeve, wipe away their tears.

Paul J Vowles

GAMBIT

A gambit! That's what they say,
after a cold cloudy day.
Indeed, what would you do?

A new face. Fresh meat amongst
the elite, the brave, the ace.
A spade, a jack and an ace.

Cold calculating crowds cheering
on this addiction. The fools!
Money is the new.

Green is everywhere. The young,
the old. Everyone worships it,
in this new age.

Spent on the exotic, and the cheap.
Needed for life and for death.
The rush of the green, a new day.

All shall fear it. All shall be
judged by it. Many forms
but only one meaning.

No pity, or remorse. It is
the vengeful god, and the dark reaper.
Snap! Someone's broke!

Danyal Fryer

THE MESSIANIC WOLF

Felt fedora, shabby raincoat, leather rhino whip
The wrong man, in the wrong place, at the wrong time
Titan your belts and your old threadbare purses
And prepare once again for the clash of the same

Spoon fed upon a diet of poverty and humiliation
Fertile soil for the purveyors of illusions
Radical situations call for radical solutions
The winter criminals had to pay then as scapegoats do now

A storm, a shock, violence shamelessly disguised as valour
An iron fist grasps an iron flag till iron leaches from the blood
Blood that stains glass beer mugs and chair legs alike
Witness butchers and bakers turn on red candle makers

Deluded puppet masters and king-makers conspire
The intellectual, the orator, the organiser and big hero
Just a lapdog, a hypocrite, a coward and a thief
Four wrong men, in the wrong place, at the wrong time

Awkward party animal, totalitarian teetotaller
But it's his party and they'll cry when he wants
The twin-striped vegetarian sucks on sweet squares of chocolate
Whilst in the kitchen cooks up a meat stew on which lions should choke

Blonde women, blonde children, blonde mothers adore him
Even the four-legged faithful turned out to be blonde
Garlands and petals for a warrior's welcome
Crushed into a cobblestone and like a memory they're gone

But time waits for no man, nor demon, nor monster
Oh so much to do before the cancer returns
Black death from black plague, black hearts in black jackboots
No rest for the wicked, well that's what they say

Resentful, deluded, how must the solution be concluded
Throw the gargantuan task to the foulest of minds
Is the devil in the detail or the detail in the devil?
Septicaemia from soft furnishings, seat leather and springs

Surrounded by sycophants all crowing for approval
Incompetent social climbers and two-faced white wine salesmen
Baton wielding, demented and gutless old phoneys
All united by one fear, that of telling the truth

The crumbling varg should have swapped loathing for listening
About the diminutive dictator who'd passed the century before
But foaming paranoia assured no such compos mentis
Thanks to Morel's baffling cocktails his insanity endured

Was once about the good folk, their saviour would save them
He'd carry on where the last one did fall
But in the end the shepherd deemed the whole flock unworthy
And damned each and all to burn slowly in Hell

Yeah no rugged cross, no ascendancy to Heaven
No opportunity to finish this millennial reign
His diary, a last appointment with his only friend Walther
And a shallow barbarian's crater his grave

Cyclical history breathes dead flesh unto life
How many times is it now he's been here before?
Over here, over there, different name, different culture
Here yesterday, today and tomorrow once more.

David Galvin

THE NIGHT STORM

A solitary gull hangs in the gale
As the tide pounds the fishing boats mercilessly
And clouds veil the crescent moon, huge drops
Of rain mix with the frothy spray of the sea

The storm rolls into the bay, lightning lighting
Up the black sky and illuminating the quay
All the residents hidden in their cosy cottages
Huddled by a log fire, kissing a sweetheart or maybe

Whiling away the long night hours in bed, cuddled close
And hearing the hammer of rain upon the window
Children wake and tremble at the rumble of thunder
Under the covers, next to parents, 'til the storm should go.

Jayne Wheatley

IN A CLOUD

Catch me in a cloud
with my detective head on
and a ribbon tied around my thoughts,

shake me out to dry
let my bones jangle out their history
just don't let me get caught,

wrap me in a rainbow
while the owls pry from yards away
with their archery skills, bows and arrows
they will never target me,

rewind my memories,
record over the sad parts please
delete all the pointless moments
pause me, before I'm diseased,

pop me down inside an envelope
and send me where I am needed
I will graft for smiles and hugs
not for greed,

transform me into a star
forget me how to fear
while there is nothing but pollution in the sky
I will shine the brightest
over your melting glaciers.

Craig Jonathan

THE EVOLUTIONIST'S PRAYER

Let us theorise . . .

Our DNA,
Which art inside each cell within us,
Most evolved is thy double helix form;
May the replication of thy protein codes be faithful;
May thy mutations always be strong;
For whilst our species is fit
On Earth we shall survive.

Given today our natural evolutionary advantages
Do not permit our dominant status as a species to
Cause us to allow the obliteration of our kind.
Lead us not into theft, murder or genocide
But mutate random beneficial characteristics
Which seem more in keeping with our contemporary
Frame of mind.

For genetics is our make-up,
Our nature,
And our identity,
Until that time when the viability
Of our species may be undone,
Or the earth, the sea and the sky
Shall be swallowed up
Into the magnitude of the sun.

So may we learn.

Neil Bywater

A BRIEF HISTORY OF SOUTH EASTERN ENGLAND

These meadows were all woodland once,
A maze of trunk and branch and bough.
Once druids prayed to dryads here,
But it is meadow now . . .

These farmlands were all meadow once,
Before men learnt to push the plough.
A pollen patch for honeybees,
But it is farmland now . . .

This village was all farmland once,
For growing crop and grazing cow.
Good honest soil for honest toil,
But times are changing now . . .

This suburb was a village once,
We wonder how did we allow
The town to conquer paradise?
But it is too late now . . .

Steven Purbeck Howarth

FOOT

This tiny, narrow foot will take
her to the moon and back before
she dies. Its shingle bones will soak
up every wave each tidal hour
flings up at her, and send them back
reformed. A single step, that's all,
to somersault the bones' attack
on stars light years beyond her call.
Let thought stir every stride, regard
for others' pacings match her own.
Let courage make each step unmarred
by pettiness or rude disdain,
that, from such small alignments, grace
might educate each measured pace.

Brian Lay

THE ROMANCE OF DEATH

A springtime beauty on a crisp blue morning,
Your baby lips a crimson budding rose.
I want you, to touch you, to possess you.
But not now. No, I'll wait, wait in the shadows
For a lifetime . . . or just in case.

Summer comes and you flourish in the sun,
Your figure blooming, attracting the bees.
My desire deepens, strengthens as I watch,
Watch but don't take, not yet. You're close, so close.
Your fragrance on my bones.

Finally you bear your autumn fruits,
Each as sweet, as succulent as you,
Yet you feel my presence now; you fear it.
Don't. My cloak rustles in the dark; you turn
But blame the frigid wind.

You lose your leaves to time; you shudder
Listening. Click, click. Click, click. You hear it now.
The rhythm of life; the tap of my bones
As I walk on the stones. Hush now, don't cry,
Leave that to the others,

For now is the time to sleep in my arms
As I brush your brow with a tender kiss.
Skin like parchment but a pleasure to touch.
My desire, my love, my aged young beauty.
True love lasts forever . . .

Stephanie Longhurst

DEAD MEAT

I'm ever so keen to make a go of this present incarnation;
The last one wasn't a big success.
There are people who swear in a previous life
They were movers and shakers and makers of history
But I am borderline cynical, I have to confess.
I never believe anyone who says they were Caesar or Gandhi, or some great
warrior queen,
You never seem to hear from the ordinary mortals, from the people who can only
claim to have been
Just a fruit fly, a sickly dog, a pot of yoghurt, or a Viking's wife,
I mean, compared to them, on the face of it, I had a lot of luck in my previous
life.

Because being a vulture is not necessarily what you'd call getting the short straw.
(An eagle would've been more poetic, and even a turkey's better looking)
But the views are good, the hours are great,
You can get through life without shopping and cooking.
You've got live carnage daily, no satellite or broadband fee
And - because you look so bad and taste even worse -
There's not an animal on Earth that's so perverse
As to fancy a nice bit of vulture for tea.

But call it a twist of fate or God's cruel trick,
I was a vulture cursed with vertigo,
(Couldn't so much as climb a tree,
Actually flying made me physically sick.)
And that's not all, my stomach was repulsed by the taste of meat,
Chicken Kiev, wildebeest: couldn't even touch it.
I occupied what's known in marketing as the most exclusive niche,
The only vulture to travel on foot with a raging lust for humus and quiche.

I can't exaggerate the impact of this on the social life of a vulture,
Just put yourself in the dirty black feathers and the big ugly feet
Of your average female, with two things in mind:
To find a mate and reproduce.
Above you is soaring Male Vulture A,
His wingspan is awesome, his plumage is spruce,
If vultures had knees then he'd make yours go weak.
He smells of warm blood and, as he circles above,
He's dropping antelope eyeballs direct to your beak:
This time it's for real, now you know you're in love.

Compare and contrast him with Male Vulture B,
He's hopping nervously from foot to foot.
For the sake of argument we'll call him me.
I'm trying to get a lift to the watering hole,
I can't get the sick stains out of me feathers,
I'm running after tourists clutching me bowl
Desperate to try and get 'em scared enough
So one of 'em might drop a Tupperware box
And leave me a sandwich or a bit of salad stuff.

These social handicaps were never more clear
Than when we went on holiday for a fortnight every year.
(Think Club 18-30 with corpses and guano, instead of sunburn and beer.)
We'd all pile down to Namibia, it's really unspoilt and the beaches are great,
And the local wildlife's widely known as easily the stupidest for miles.
In fact the accident-prone locals are the only reason why
Namibia is the number one vulture destination;
They don't care about the beaches and the lovely clean air
So much as quantity of roadkill and a nice bit of sun.
(If Bath was 100 in the shade with a dead horse very mile,
Then provided they could park they'd probably end up there.)

Anyway, the thing about Namibia is,
It's where it's at for vulture sex,
And if you're not flying down, then you're not getting any;
And it's no good hitching, no one picks up a vulture.
Drivers always think you'll get droppings on the seat
And the buses are infrequent and half of them don't stop.
And if they do, the driver says, 'Oi! Vulture! You're sitting on the top!
Or if you are coming in, then I'm going to charge you double
Cos no one's going to want to have to share a seat with you.'

And OK, alright, this one time I did have a little spot of trouble.
Old fella on the back seat; he seemed dead enough to me.
I'm sorry, but if you're as old as that *and* not snoring, then
                                            it's really hard to tell.
Plus his tongue was all dried up and it was definitely already loose as well.

I don't think I've picked up any wisdom or absorbed any lessons
Since the driver chucked me off that bus and I perished beneath a passing Jeep.
The only lingering traces of my former existence are the contours of my nose
Plus a slight fear of heights and undercooked meat and a tendency to weep
Grateful tears of joy whenever I find a lover who likes someone
To nibble hard on her fingers, ears and toes.
In fact all potential partners are issued with a warning
Which comes with a promise which they're well advised to keep,
If you're next to me at night and keen to see another morning,
Then fidget, snore, do what you must; just never lie still when you fall asleep.

Jez Prins

THE WIND'S INSTIGATION

The wind speaks to me.
It roars and rattles, unsettles the house.
I think of you.
The briefness of our touch,
The sliding of one person's hand against another.
Snatched.
A quickly captured moment,
A quick moment taken away.
Someone's eyes on us.
The wind thunders gain.
My heart glides at the thought of you
Or floats happily at the mention of your name, or
The thought of us together.
I love you, I love you,
I love you!
I just know it.
But, perhaps it is the wind.
The loquacious ways of the Earth.
Time to sleep; to rest in nature.
The wind awakens us all.
Still, I want to touch your heart.
Write my name across it forever, like a star in the sky.

Maria Stebbing

MEMORY

I stand outside your window
Waiting,
To see the face I never forgot.
A foggy haze
Inside this diminished heart,
Tangled with my broken thoughts.
Lost,
In this entwining chasm
Of thorns,
The misery of life without you brings.
Mental divisions
Keep your face locked away.
Tears shape the reflections
Of your soul
In the broken mirror,
Below.
You lie wistlessly beyond
My memory.
Out of reach.
My memory,
A shimmering spectre
On the precipice
Of real.

Claire Adams

PEACE TIME

Ancient sentinels stand their bare-armed watch,
Flanking fields badged with mud.
Once taunted from behind barbed wire front lines,
Head hunkered private sheep their vigil keep,
Midst tin and packet.
Accompanied by a crow-called fanfare,
Their realm defended.

Jonathan Daniels

THE UNREALITY

Life distracts
As I, obtuse,
Diffused and detached
Deconstruct.

The glue has come unstuck.

As I who drown in a sea of sounds
That rebound from invisible walls
Scream scripted speech against the tide
Into the blue
Blurred bordered
Linear
Without a within.

True, the veil has dropped
Like a fallen shadow.
Like
Falling
Snow.

And I am alone.

And these eyes are not my own.
And these hands are not my own.

And all is glass and stone.

Kelly Page

UNTITLED

Where sounds seeped, I went forth
Beneath a sky of tender thoughts
And there in the fields of syllables lost
I ate the fruits of the vine
Noticing not the clouds above me
Replenishing the rivers below
Flowing like a dream 'neath the stars I sleep
Languishing not on the stings of guilt
I'm running through a field of verbenas.

Philip John Traynor

UNTITLED

The image has haunted me all my life.
The body reduced down to its inner core and horror frame.

Flesh and muscle hang - worn and weak, translucent and thin,
Clinging to the horror like loose scaffolding -
Ready to be peeled away, easily - like melted cheese.

Withered to its root, surrounded by the dead,
Which fill deep ditches, dark and overloaded carts.
She has survived, somehow - survives this horror, this hell,
To witness sweet liberation - freedom from this unspeakable.
A blessing from above - the angels have come . . .

Weak and dying, barely moving, but filled with hope -
She is asked to stand, and pose -
And this new devil demands, 'Say cheese.'

One last task, one last job for the innocent -
But -
        Work will set you free.

Richard Green

CHERISHED SENSES

I see you in a fold of silk, the one you wore on sunny days
and from the brush you used each night,
I touch a silver wisp of hair.

Here in the room I smell your scent,
in all the places that you passed
and hear again that 'tinkling' smile,
that lingers deep so placed with care.

And oh so deep within this heart,
that stays confined as form dictates,
I taste the kiss that sealed our love
and cherish it to keep it there.

Tom Martin

VETERAN OF WAR

The drunken veteran of war lays his sorrows
to rest amidst the liquor
His face is hardened stone, weathered by
the grains of time in the desert.
He's sat in a hardened posture, brow furled
reminiscing the dread sound,
As bullets tear through the silence of night,
disturbing his dreary sleep.
This place was dead, like the victims and
comrades who had fallen in a bleak cause.
A flurry of wild passion fuelled by a drive of religious warring.
Each grain of sand is a lost soul condemned
to the heat, the dehydration.
The lust for blood which is only slaked
by the mad recompense of the pilgrim.
The smoke in the room stung his eyes.
His dirty khaki camouflage jacket, standard issue,
was faded and discoloured with age.
He gulped the harsh liquid deadening the
living breathing noxious fumes.
Nothing to show and nothing to hide,
lost in the media's coverage.
A faceless soldier not praised or acknowledged
for his deeds once home.
Yet we stir so egregiously with gargantuan hunger
waiting to devour the next piece of propaganda.
Eyeless, dogless and carnivorous.

The eyes that become glassy after life has slipped from them
look blankly at the stars.
Lost dreams of a now dead man, never to
father a child or bear a wife.
Grief-stricken and helpless, the repercussions
seize friend and relatives,
brothers and brothers alike.
As a terrorist holding a group of children hostage.
But when we look to the world, its problems fall on our doorsteps.
Bereft of ownership and a cowardly scent left in the hasty retreat,
fleeing from a shadow of a tyrannical war crime.
Look within our town, our own community, our own worlds.
Our own problems outweigh the bigger ones here.
Poverty is the working class.

But lest we solve the 'issues' passed down by our forefathers,
how are we to help others?
Addictive drugs bring a populous dependant on nothing,
as long as they ask no questions.
You will tell us no lies.

The media like the moon at night watch
and devour the atrocities of the black.
The sounds that ring in the silence,
tearing the long stretches of dunes.
But as we dust our shelf, his merit is lost
in the erosion of chemical polish,
his friends' faces blurred and distorted, his tears roll.
1984.

Stephen Shimmans

CARTHAGE

Phoenician faces, almost Grecian
Stare in wide-eyed wonder
At the weary twentieth-century traveller
As he blunders through the arid ancient sites
Cowering under Apollo's blistering gaze,
Eyes screwed tightly shut against his piercing rays.
Peering intently, almost touching the sun-baked mosaics.
Cheek to cheek with the Phoenician sailors
As they glide in their golden galleons
Across their stony ocean.

Dark-eyed Numidian nymphs in secret trysts peep shyly
From underneath their black-fringed lashes,
Frozen in stone, blasted by the sands of time;
Locked forever in another dimension
Like dragonflies in amber.
Knowing how long they've waited there
We kneel and stroke their matted hair.

Rusty Woodward Gladdish

FOR WHAT?

Most ordinary men labour hard all their life
Tending for children and for their wife . . .
For them each new day brings toil and more
A bigger worry than the one before . . .

Bills to pay . . . work to do . . .
Another day to battle through . . .
Where will it end? Is it in sight?
Can the cursed slog be put to fight?

Can they not get their share
Of life's sweet riches that for others are everywhere?
Now let's ask! 'Who will honestly help the ordinary man?'
To at least harvest some wealth wherever he can.

And not deny a single soul their equal right
As seen through the logic of the creator's own true light . . .

But work it is to have and to hold
To make them grey before they are old . . .
Never a thought of quality here
Only a token illusion dangled near

That finally fool nor compensate
For the reward of forced toil at a hectic pace

The tragedy is now for all to see
Ordinary women are now trapped so blatantly . . .

'Mundane', once the domain of the working man
Is now the shackle of the working woman . . .
And in the name of freedom she has walked in crimson drape . . .
To the place where ordinary men were desperate to escape . . .

For what? . . . For what? I ask, as countless others before . . .
What do we really need with all this?
More and more . . .
With freedom comes responsibility and choice
But where is the freedom for those with no voice?
Their responsibilities are stacked sky high
By those who want the biggest slice of the pie!

Those such as bankers and lords get the biggest crust.
Only ordinary people do what they must . . .
To pay what is needed to keep them fed
And through the lure of more . . . walk the path of the living dead.

A wise Red Indian was once heard to say. . .
'If this is progress, let us rue this day.'
Be warned! Be warned! If our sole ambition is to beat the rest,
It will be our final and ultimate test.

Our kind shall surely rot from within
And the buzzards above us shall eat our skin
And the taste of Armageddon we shall tell
As lured we are into living Hell . . .

To try our best is a human goal!
To be the best don't sell your soul!
To win at any cost is not to win
When you forfeit the respect of kith and kin!

Ordinary talk should have power indeed . . .
For they satisfy many of their avarice and greed!
The manipulator's plan is a simple ploy
Make him and her work for a trinket and toy!
Throw them some crumbs and they'll be fine
As the ordinary line up in an orderly line . . .
Epilogue . . . The simple truth . . .

Those with agendas are not to be sought
Those with needs are fed up with nought
Angry ordinary folk who were willing to reckon
Have sold their soul for a rich man's beckon

And will not condemn what is obviously wrong
In words or protests is a great protest song . . .
Complacency is rife . . . the die it is cast
I pray this plea will not be the last!

Chris Redfern

ADA MARGUERITTE

I think of spring's first crocus display,
so short a time since we were wed.
My husband's life was taken away.

While birdsong resounds in the day,
sorrows lie in the trenches ahead.
I think of spring's first crocus display.

Guns are muffled far away,
so many words remain unsaid.
My husband's life was taken away.

'Don't give up hope,' the comrades say,
praying for their lives to be spared.
I think of spring's first crocus display.

Flesh is grass, foreign fields grey,
white daisies shroud the regiment's dead.
My husband's life was taken away.

War graves dug out, poppies sway,
obedient, we were willingly led.
I think of spring's first crocus display,
my husband's life was taken away.

Margaret Quilter

RESEMBLANCE

I watch you staring back at me
Your hazel eyes soaked through with tears,
Their only harvest - enmity,
I watch you staring back at me.
You sowed the seeds, but killed the tree
And now you weep across the years.
I watch you staring back at me
Your hazel eyes soaked through with tears.

Leonie Martin

FEEDING ROOKS

He swings in like a pirate
from topmast rigging
clearing the decks of smaller fry.
Swaying importantly
in this conquered space
he slashes at the treasure
with sharp curved glints.
His mates muscle in
on the booty
and their deep rough shouts
bring more.

Glamour and power drip glossily
from their loose apparel.
Waves of shining black
slide and shift.
Cutlasses skilfully deploy
as they seize their prize
and hold the bridge
against all-comers.

This winter, enemies
brought down their high cradles.
Burned their boats.

But they are back
crow's-nesting twig by twig
moss-lining tenderly.
There will be new notes
in the old sea shanty.
Rookies to the pirate trade.

Linna Monteath

WHITE APRIL

The night you looked so frail and supple.
The night you crossed your legs.
Whilst the blond boy came with apples.
Whilst the blond boy begged and bled.

O dearest white April, in the churchyard you saw
My pale pleasure sighing as you lay on the floor.
As you begged me inside, it was fear, and not pride
That so suddenly dismantled my heart and then died.

O dearest white April, in the city we slept,
And they watched but back then, in a black box I was kept.
My morning, my evening, my day and my night,
You were the sun; my life and my light.

O dearest white April, these green fingers come.
They crawl through my skin and like legs, they can run.
I can cover both eyes like stars the night skies,
But like ten million spiders, they're all fat with lies.

O dearest white April, please listen to me!
The faces - they all have now started to see.
The cracks and the lines in their skin and their smiles
Like long and deep lakes that leave you sinking for miles.

O dearest white April, please hear when I say,
Every soldier did die, before he went away.
And in mid spring, when we loved by the lake,
Like small silhouettes, the moon we did take.

O dearest white April, in the ocean we swam,
Do you remember being naked and cold in the sand?
Do you remember falling upon green grass by the sea?
Do you remember whispering that you felt so free?
O dearest white April . . . do you remember me?

Those nights when making love stang
And the tepid sheets clung to your shins and
They were a hot, cold prison.
And upon War's oily, opaque, unkillable legs I walked.
Flesh can't be fixed. Love can't be taught.

O dearest white April, thrust your wrists in the water,
And pour them away like men do their daughters.
When we danced in the dunes and we spoke and we smiled,
Like we weren't two silk tents in a thin, floating world.

O dearest white April, through old skin I breathe,
The cold's in my bones and I'm frightened to leave.
For it is Time who conquers all, not Love I fear,
And it is with this subtle foe, we will all disappear.

O dearest white April, please don't be alarmed
At these thin purple threads that have crawled up my arms.
The lake and our love are long in the past,
Long gone are those slithers, good things never last.

Like the pier with sand beneath the wooden tracks,
Like the smell of the rain on the concrete and cracks,
Like the people in houses with hot, hollow eyes,
Like the trenches with swarms of screaming black flies.

Now, neither pen nor rain could drip a sea
To sail me back through time to be
With you, so it is here I'll drift
Etiolated in lost love's mist.

O dearest white April, it was when I came home,
That I did not know what to become,
So I became alone.

O dearest white April, in case you can't see,
I was the blond boy who begged. He was me.

Alex Taylor

IDENTITY

Faith captured in a gloom of rain
Torn apart in the sound of wind
Scared off by its own beings
Tempted by its own kind
Dared upon humanity
Every second became a fight
No sacred purity is blessed regarding such heights
Vanity and integrity stood by it still
Thirst and anger both took sides
Minds triggered to conceive
As harmony began to strike
Loneliness forgotten as a pain
Fate took another side . . .

Tajmina Begum Miah

CATSEYES VS CANDLELIGHT

Flowing, frosted, white garments accentuate
an ornate window display
Like the perfect arch guarding,
cosmetic art frames an ethereal face
And through the skylight, a playground of imagination
matures and ripens to amber
Mimicking the introversion of a tired sunset,
as the refreshed sunrise follows a calculated life number.

Catseyes resemble hazy candle lights,
radiating a blazing trail on a dusky roadside.
The stars patrolling the north parade spit fireworks
high into a shivering, satin sky.
A ceasefire celebration of a volatile expression
converting to the religion of nature's tune.
A path so romanticised, it's the only way to gain
the attention and highlight of the grand cosmic room.

Fabricate a cascade of mirrored images,
so there's a dimension to leave behind.
The inferno ignites to be desired,
the desire burns to be inspired, but by a different kind.
A secret feels new, always multiple and transparent.
But no destination will ever be reached so blind.
A shared summer realisation is a spark
from an enigma, we've misunderstood.
Translate the answers, disclosed as
a time-reflected, midnight flood.

Samantha Webb

SEND

email hotmail
surf and text
SMS an SOS
hi-technology
new strain of sociology

mobile magic
cool and ease
word perfect geek-speak
quick communication
communicomputerisation

high impact, low contact
just words

no one's unavailable
easy access
more is less

and if distance doesn't matter
may as well be on another planet

no tactile sensation
in this speed communication
this technology
an apology for biology

when all I want to do is
skin to skin and breath to breath
and voice to voice round throwaway words
sounds only, saying more.

Jane Davies

I NEVER WANTED

I never wanted a white horse
Some kind of fairy tale
I didn't ask for beautiful pearls
You felt like I'd made you steal the sun
Just to have a nice day

We spoke to each other
But our ears were deaf
Sharp tongues on thin air
It felt like I'd asked you
To write it all down

The picture never got finished
We had to put water in the paint
To keep the brush strokes
I wish you had put the sun in that sky

I never wanted that red dress
Some kind of romance
I didn't ask for roses or forget-me-nots
You felt like I'd made you
Light up the stars just for a nice evening

We glanced at each other
But our eyes were distant
Hands that once held us together
You felt like I'd asked you
To never leave my side

Colours smudged and bled
We tried to clean up, we messed up
We got dirty hands
I wish we could have enjoyed
What we painted together.

Kathryn Fieldhouse

NO REBEL

You say that I am 'a rebel without a cause'
with my high-top boots,
my death metal groups,
my long hair sheen,
my left wing lean,
you say that I have no reason to complain
or anything to profane,
a pacifist in wars,
a rebel with no cause.

I say to you I am no rebel, nor would I want to be,
a rebel is an incomplete man, lost in himself, not free,
he fights the conservatives of this world,
with their brandy, cigars and crosses unfurled,
yet when the rebel wins his war he
can do little but light a cigar, sip brandy, and vote Tory.

You say that I am 'a rebel without a cause',
Perhaps. I fight no wars, settle no scores.
I say to you that I am a corrupter of words,
a watcher of worlds. So stop staring.
These boots will trample you,
these metal groups will be the death of you,
this hair will hide your face,
this leaning will push you over the edge.

You say that I am 'a rebel without a cause',
at least I'm not a rebel without balls.

Chris Page

MICHAEL'S MESS

Shrieking, the woman
slithers to the perfume counter,
fingernails splayed out
like a spider with patent shoes.
Shapely bottles
cascade, clattering;
fragrance escaping
their broken bodies.

The reluctant skater
with wrinkling nose
leans among surviving bottles,
wiping her stilettos.
She glares
at the spreading puddle
that caused her collision,
and Michael's trousers, dripping.

My invisible shell closes around:
a twenty-year-old protection
from opinions of people
who don't understand.

Pink-clothed women
hurry to the scene
equipped with smiles, mops
and 'wet floor' cones.
As I roll up his trousers
to fix his catheter,
Michael leans over,
grunting his laughter.

Cleaning the wheelchair,
I notice his smile
caught and returned
by the girl shovelling glass.
Michael's eyes:
dark lash-framed doorways,
welcoming people
into his soul.

In his open-eyed world,
simple glories of life
are noticed and lifted
from humdrum existence:
miniature flowers
tucked into stone walls;
shapes in the clouds;
and Gordon's echo.

Wishing again
that Michael's father
had lived to see
our longed-for baby,
I realise now
that through Gordon's death
was born my resolve
to keep his child.

An elderly woman
shoves a bag in my hands
mumbling 'Oxfam';
I peek inside, and understand.
Michael delights
in his flowery trousers,
ignoring the looks
on the way home.

The mess isn't Michael's.
Around him, it happens
in the chaos created
by rushing through life,
in the tangle of hang-ups,
the wrinkling worry
that so many carry
in crowded heads.

In his uncluttered mind
life is precious;
beauty is everywhere;
he is loved.

I shall never forget
my grandmother's words
as she stroked his face
in that first, precious hold.
His fragile frame cradled
in her hands, arthritic,
her gaze, for a second,
caught my son's.

'Listen to this baby, Lisa,'
she murmured softly,
'let him teach you
about life.'
And through two decades
infused with stress, sorrow, sweetness,
I realise, so much,
how right she was.

Janet White

APGAR SCORE

There was a final tearing wrench
Before we went from one to two.
They held you up in alien air
And took you for a minute.
Then they placed you on my skin.
I smiled, uncertainly, for the camera;
You turn your squashed-up face away
And in to me, as though to tunnel back in.
I didn't know what to do
So I cried, I think;
And you cried, I think.
But somehow we muddled through.
Soon they took you from me again,
And did some things to that tiny you:
Weighed and measured and judged.

On display in that glass box
You passed your first tests.

Theresa Gooda

HE-SHE

He, she are aged beyond their years,
no hope . . . no future . . . no existence
except one of unrelenting, unforgiving toil
He is old and bent with resignation,
She with lifeless, wizened breasts
That once nourished children now dead.
They cling, exist, together
not from love, but necessity
in an uncaring world.
Why, what have they done,
what is their crime?
And the answer is, nothing.
Nothing except to be born in a place
where existence is just existence,
born to live, to toil, to die,

sans end.

Whilst in other parts of the world
people pile possessions on waste tips,
shop 'til they drop and then go for more,
eat until they are obese and then spend to slim.
Unfair? - Not to the many for whom
the pangs of hunger mean little.
But in the darkness which seems to gather ever closer
is there hope of a brighter day of he and she
before we face a night of everlasting self-oblivion?
The answer is yes, when we learn to share
to give, to care, to love, to forget self,

the answer lies with you and me!

Ron Sweeney

HEROES

This cold cuts through the hardest men.
The ruthless reminder - the sun shall expose us again.
The darkness that cloaks our Soul is ripped away by the Dawn,
Mocking,
Reducing Might and Glory to distant Dreams.
Where are they? Those that stood Tall
Climbing to Victory,
With only Passion,
Strength,
Unity?
Did our spirit fall for this Light?
And the poetry of the Robin
The smell of Glory
And the taste of fresh new dairy?
Neighbours greet and wish us Paradise.
Her enthusiasm is repulsive
From a universe of Joy and Ecstasy.
We too danced to that melody
And our neighbour dreamt of eggs and coffee.
The Battle was won, the possibilities infinite.
A Thief crept in and stole our Prize,
Our game was weak, yesterday's news.
The Agony, the Remorse
Oh the shame.
The Looking Glass portrays Hideous Reflections of the Heart.
But wait . . .
To Crumble in the jaws of Adversity never drove us to Overwhelming Heights.
The Haven holds a Secret,
We remain Faithful, search and strive
For the Gift that lies in All Places,
Of the gold we held so close, so tight.
And we shall Clutch it once more,
Today!
No time for Breakfast, for Fuel,
No time for expired Symphonies,
The orchestra lunges Heroes into gear,
Relentless,
Unforgiving.
Prepare.
The Day grows Bright.
And so shall we,

Higher than ever before.
A simple leap of Faith or more,
For that which is Alien?
Authentic Soul.
No Trickery, away with the Promise of War.
This Day we Present Heart.
Lord, how We Triumph.

Ferdi Mehmet

PERSONALITIES POURING FROM AN OPEN WINDOW

The sound of acceptance, the traffic builds,
The engines hum a tune.
The sound of Dylan, the rock of Springsteen,
The openness, the room.
The tapping, the revving, the ambience and fresh air,
The rocking beat, the country folk,
The music of Gallagher.
The sunshine and open windows,
Exposed elbows and nodding heads,
The individuality, the motorbikes, the vans with beds.
Surrounded, lonely, assigned to a lane
Cirrostratus, milky-white veil, a chance of rain.
Separated by law, restricted by space,
Confined to a box, unable to race.
A snail's trail of traffic, dancing fingers aloft,
A field of colour, burning rubber so soft.
Denied anonymity, home sometime tonight,
Job of the day to accept the plight.
No room to move, no chance to stand,
A sea of traffic in need of land.
A moving car park, entry fee to go,
Personalities pouring from an open window.

Janet Millard

FOR BETTER, FOR WORSE

Where was she?
Time was slipping away.
It had taken him hours to cycle
On his rickety bike to the small
Church on the hill.
The chain kept jumping,
Was it telling him to stop and think?
Both tyres, riding on their rims,
Flat as pancakes.
He checked the two brass curtain rings
For the hundredth time.
All he could find at such short notice
And adjusted his Highland uniform.

Home on leave from desert fighting,
His short visit had been filled
With frenetic arrangements.
He had borrowed loose change
For the church scramble.
In fact, he had borrowed everything.
He could still see her eyes sparkle
When he asked her to marry him,
Yet, she had panicked. There would be
No time to organise anything special.
The rationing made sure of that.
Would she still come?
He loved her so much.
Her mother had spent all night
Cutting up old papers
Into small pieces for confetti.
A simple cake was baked, no icing
Small decorations made from food labels
And any coloured paper she could find.
Neighbours chipped in with soup,
Sandwiches and small bakes
For the wedding meal to be held
In the back garden.
Old sheets were cut up to make
Her wedding dress.
This dress was to be sewn on to her
And would be cut off for dusters afterwards.
She felt like her grandma's tailor dummy,

Yet she felt rather pretty.
Flowers were picked from the garden
And made into small bouquets,
Their petals sprinkled onto her hair.
Old net screens were made into a veil
She was the perfect bride.

It would be a quick reception.
Today was booked solid
With soldiers and their sweethearts
Waiting in line, just like a factory
Conveyor belt.
The hall looked like the deck of a sloping
Battleship on a stormy sea
Empty then full, full then empty.
As she walked down to meet him,
She felt good.
Today the world would marry them
Whether they were ready or not.
Tomorrow the world would separate them
Whether they wanted it or not.

Next morning found them standing
On the railway platform.
He gave her a small keepsake.
'Keep it safe, I won't need this
Where I'm going.'
'Take care,' she whispered.
'Don't worry, this is one person
Hitler won't get,' he said.
She clasped the withered red rose
In her hand and kissed it.

She found herself, years later
Standing on the same platform
Clutching the dried red rose.
Was he on the last train?
Did she see his smile?
The train emptied and she turned
To leave. Her heart heavy.
What would she do now?
The war had ended,

Peace had come without him.
Suddenly, she felt a warm hand
Searching for her fingers.
He was home and she was in his arms.

Josephine Duthie

I STAND ALONE

Time ticks and ticks,
Every second the drip of a rusty tap,
Hollow desolate landscape,
A desert of words held fast and bleak in the dusty space.
You could not look me in the eye,
The wall held your focus for so long,
The clock chimed an interruption,
You glanced at my face,
Made an attempted quip,
Were you scared that I would cry or speak truths unwanted?
Time, such time and no time,
So many rights, for me no wrongs,
But for you who knows?
When silence binds your soul,
And that wall, that wall I so despise,
Remains unpeeling
Tick, tick, tick . . .
I love you
To distraction,
What else can I ask of you?
Love me back, perhaps less than some,
Just for myself and that will do!

Sarah Kent

CHAIN REACTION

First she was skipping,
then she was dangerously tripping,
next she was disastrously falling,
loudly calling,
hoping that someone would be there
to stop and care
enough
to stoop
then scoop her
from the rough
ground,
responding to her sound.

The boys in the playground heard
her every word
but she remained visually unobserved.
Those boys talked of Beckham,
the demise from the Premiership of West Ham
as well as other issues concerning football.
At last they turned, but all they did was stand and stare,
it was too late, they had ignored her call.

Neill Cadmore

ON WATCHING THREE OLD DRINKERS

And whose are these eyes
Sunk in thick-brimming liquid oblivion?
And whose are these mouths
Uncontrollable rubber bands,
Chewing on unspoken words
They spit tasteless back in the glass?
Leaning in putrid puddles
On mahogany counters of gloom,
Their overwound heads tick-tock on
Like the springs of an open clock
Until closing time,
When their lonely souls
Throw silent shadows in the lamplight.

Kim Russell

BROKEN THINGS

Tired
Receding dignity and hairline
Receding respect now you're an elder
The shakes, the trembles, vacant looks
Yet it all is locked in yet is seeping away
Through unseen holes day by day
Memories like photos fade
Until the images barely carry any shape
Points of recollection - get moved
Points of recollection - get lost
Among this filing cabinet of the cranium
There's an undoubted sadness for them
But they are thankfully removed from the sense
There's an undoubted sadness for those
Who watch and try to tend such wounds
They fruitlessly try to stem the tide of time
As its daily engagement recedes ever further
For those marooned on beaches such as these
They'll never make it back to the flowing waters
They'll remain beyond the lapping waves
The aches, the pains, the daily doses of pills
These broken things were once people
Yet their hearts still beat strong and steady
It's their minds that have beat the retreat
No longer capable of communicating
They live within a slowed down world
That merely tracks the day and night
No chinks in this armour, no given clue
For those who tend, for those who care
Born out of the tie that blood can bind
You mop their distant brow
You squeeze the hand and search for
The faintest glimmer that they're aware
Of the concern and love that cannot
Truly tough the heart for whatever
Roadblocks stop the messages
Transmitted being received and
Comprehended - to be so close

Yet to seem so distant as if you were
Worlds away - and you pause to recall
When you metered out harsh words
Unaware of the descent and decline.

Richard Gould

THE FINAL HOURS

Death impatiently hovered outside my door,
I have a silver casket for your lad
'Take your black steeds and leave us,
Whilst he still has breath you shall not take him.'
Very well, but I will return soon,
Fate cannot be cheated.

I cradled my angel's head and wiped his eyes,
His fur was brushed once more.
Gently and softly I spoke to him,
'You will be so handsome when it is time for your journey.
I have loved you to the depths of my heart
And that will always be so.'

All our memories danced through my head
And teased me.
For what had passed between us would be no more.
I cuddled your frail body in my lap
And gave thanks for your unswerving love.

My sorrow knew no bounds, as my tears fell
I quickly wiped them from your pristine fur.
Then there it was, the haunting hammer on my door
Stoically you gave your last breath
As your life was no more.

Theresa Carrier

HOW TO GET DOLPHINS BACK INTO TREES

'I don't like dolphins stuck in trees,'
Said Horace, far too hard to please;
'In poetry, as in plastic art
From the real world you'll take your start.
Surrealist fantasies are banned;
You can't have dolphins on the land;
With censure editorial
Cut out their kind arboreal!'
But the young Ovid came along,
A master of subversive song,
And put them back a clever way,
Almost too obvious to say:
He had a great flood, like the Bible,
Where he'd be playful and describe all
The accidents of that event,
With things outside their element;
And in that flood he had some dolphins,
Sporting and clapping with their small fins,
And soon within his new-made seas
He had them bumping into trees.

Graham Anderson

THE RISEN HOPE

If I could only touch the stars
And feel the splendour of up above
My heart would rest content
That Thy greatness is the mere epitome of love

Would my pain only melt away
And sink into the deep abyss of truth
I would not have did what I did
And neither would I have said 'I would'

For no mortal bequeaths me his torments to bear
The hope of salvation steers in my mind
The transparency of faith lies opaque before my eyes
The outcome of fate a mystery untwined.

Margaret Bakajika

PARTING

How hard it is to leave you when we part!
Each rendezvous, each murmuring of the heart
With speed are gone,
And in their stead
The ache of emptiness
Wherein not even angels dare to tread!

Those golden moments all alone we share
They're but too fleeting fully to enjoy.
Yet soul meets soul, increasingly aware
Of empathy too special to destroy,
And heightened senses wistfully foresee
How passionate, how tender love could be.

Too soon - in feeble guise -
Time's fickle feet move on.
Each minute we're together swiftly flies,
The interlude was here and now is gone.
The stage lies bare.
Two spirits left
Bereft.

For separation ever hovering there -
Nor welcome, nor invited to attend -
Intrudes with calm and calculating chill
To bring an end -
And leave us longing still.

So when shall next we meet?
Next month? Next week? Tomorrow?
What unknown age must pass, what joy, what sorrow?
For now a silent hug, a wave goodbye,
With all the cheer reluctant hearts can feign;
Inside, unheard, a hollow cry
And such familiar pain . . .

Verity Gill Malkinson

WHERE LEGENDS BEGAN

Let me take you - if I may - along the path where bluebells stray
outside the walls of Carmarthen - the source of legends here began.

Forest deep and life so still -
just imagine - if you will:

A sunbeam - through the crowns of oak -
gently touches crimson cloak.

A pony's hooves distracts the peace - a ring dove from its shelter flees,
the rider young - just mere a child - catches glimpse of the falcon in flight.

The path now climbing - bracken breast high,
cliffs hung with ivy - almost touching the sky.

Rabbits scatter and hide underground -
a trickle of water the only sound.

The boy dismounts and climbs the rock -
and legend tells of a wooden god.

The last time this carved figure he'd seen -
was under the oak at Tyr Myrddin.

And by the spring he fills the cup -
and quenches his thirst -and that of his god.

And watched by the falcon he enters the cave-
not sure of his feelings - not feeling unsafe.

Torches were guiding his way underground -
a child's curiosity - the crystal cave found.

And millions of diamonds bursting with light,
rainbows and rivers and stars shining bright.

Crimson dragons clawing the wall -
and below him a face - of a girl growing tall.

Gently he closes his eyes to see -
and light enters body - to set his mind free.

There before him bearded and grey,
a tall figure stood waiting for his arrival today.

A wizard? A hermit? A holy man? -
Nobody knows - but legend began.

And witness to this were the cave's resting bats,
when he says, 'I'm your teacher Galapas.'

And moons followed suns and days turned to night
and wisdom grew - and the boy gained sight.

And as Myrrdin Emrys the boy was known -
those were the years when Merlin was born.

And Galapas taught him all that he knew - and the falcon stayed -
'til at last - he once more again flew.

And Myrrdin Emrys - now Merlin by name - alongside Ambrosius -
created Arthur - and long they did reign.

And if I may - for one moment alone -
drift back to the cave created by stone,
and leadeth you through darkness to light -
to the crystal that shimmers like diamonds bright -
and can you see what I see through my looking glass?
Then you must hear the infinite wisdom of Galapas:

The gods only go with you - if you put yourself in their path!

And now friends go forth - tell legend to child and remember -
when your eyes pass - a falcon in flight.

Regina Widd

DRINK

I look at you, what's in your head?
I offer companionship, you'll have a drink instead.
I long for love, and ordinary things,
You'll reach for a drink and the numbness it brings.
The distance between us is widening I fear,
I'm crying out for attention, lost in drink you don't hear.
The children need us as much as they did,
But you reach for a drink and de-cap the lid.
'We need help, get help!' is all I can shout.
You say, 'I need a drink, I'm going out.'
Conscience, respect, there's nowhere to go,
Drink's deceitful charms are all that you know.
My family, my home, are slipping away,
But reeking of drink, in you sway,
Then ice hits glass with a sickening familiar clink,
I'll never compete with this mistress called drink.

Geraldine Donnelly

WINGS ON A PRAYER

(In loving memory of my wife)

Fly, my little osprey, fly
above the tossing, tumbling swell
of textbook fears and ne'er do well,
that highway there and back from Hell
and pulsate on a ticking bell.

Fly above those make-up wires
and broken Hollywood desires,
across the realms of clear blue sky
on wings that stretch to catch
each current's hope, and breathe
the freshest southern mountain air
that takes us on to God knows where.

You've come through the skyscraping
fashions, fads, pressures and ads
of the fast moving danger-filled
hustle and bustle of capital life.
And you've skirted the treetops,
the fields and the hedgerows,
and dived the fresh waters
to pull out the fish.
You've reflected the twinkle
that shines from each star,
and you've joined in the rhythm
of the New Orleans mardi gras.

And now my one remaining wish
is that you'll take your deepest breath
and spread your wings across the sea
above the tides of blue and green,
my lovely Caribbean queen.
My God reveal His love to you
and carry your tired form upstream
to bring you safely home to me.

Julian Collins

THE BEGGARS IN PENNILESS PORCH

Kill Canon Corner is always cold
As the wind gusts round the stony cliffs
Of the cathedral in Wells.

The beggars are out in Penniless Porch
But sniffing and drinking,
Smoking and singing
Is never enough to keep them warm.
So they shiver and leap
And cough and sleep
In their beds of boxes broadsheet and blankets;
They hug themselves in their battered clothes
And they put their hats at our feet.

These fag-ends of people
Are not what we want
In a cathedral close.
Let us draw in our skirts, then, and button our coats,
Keep ourselves clean and warm and apart -
But just suppose
That we are the beggars in Penniless Porch,
Knocking at Heaven's door?

Do we know we are poor?
Do we know what beggars we are
In the haven of Penniless Porch?
Let us plead for ourselves then,
Put down our hats
And beg for ourselves in Penniless Porch,
Knocking at Heaven's door.
For there unseen in the place of our poverty,
Unexpected, small and surprising,
Jesus is waiting to let us in.

Margaret Sparshott

ST GEORGE'S DAY

Eight there at table; I the host -
St George's Day, by chance.
The chatter ran through soup and roast.
With cheese, we turned to France.
Old Calais once was ours, you know?
We knew. Not much, but that;
just as we knew the world was round.
Nobody bid for flat.

Things French led to Italians
who also liked to hide
when bombs and bullets flew about.
Great, on the other side.
We slagged the Germans, as you do,
and tutted at the Dutch.
Weren't they on our side, World War Two?
Yes, but not very much.

The port brought up the Portuguese;
no wrong that they could do.
Our oldest allies, don't you know?
Yes, we all knew that too.
Our tour of Europe's' shortcomings
burned up the Fulham night
and then we talked of England.
No surprise; we thought we might.

And I it was who raised a glass -
'Saint George!', but not too loud,
and added how come Scots and Welsh
and Irish did theirs proud
while we the English kept it dark
or maybe didn't know
the twenty-third of April was
our day. Why was that so?

I swore it wasn't good enough!
The booze was talking now -
and talking as I thought befit
a kind old tawny Dow.
I cursed presenters who sat on
those bloody breakfast shows
with shamrock'd, thistle'd, leek'd lapels!

Why don't we wear our rose?

A lady sitting three along
leaned forward, turned to me.
She didn't say that she agreed.
She didn't disagree,
but spoke one line which brought a chill
of silence to we few.
(I swear I heard Drake's drum)
She said . . . , 'Perhaps *we* don't need to.'

Waterman Quill

THE UNFORGIVABLE SIN

Seventy times seven
And the first of the seventy first
Is when we will not be forgiven, my love -
The first of the seventy first.

Seventy times seven times
Have we sinned against our fathers
This is the first of the seventy first -
This is the first of the seventy first.

Seventy times seven times
Have we climbed on this Brokeback Mountain
The first of the seventy first, my love -
This is the first of the seventy first.

Seventy times seven times
Have we turned from light to black -
This is the first of the seventy first
This is the first of the seventy first.

Seventy times seven
And the first of the seventy first
Is when we will not be forgiven, my love . . .
This is the first of the seventy first.

Tanya Aksarova

RUN OVER

This is pressing,
This feeling of being squashed,
My moisture spurting in particles across cement.
What a way to end up.
A two dollar rose meant for a teenage love,
Bought at a gas station;
My peasant start does not make me lack pride,
But what a way to end up.
It's painful, like a human heart shattering;
My former wielder's organ of emotion crushed through me.
Flowers, especially red roses can't cry,
Yet I moan in tones that no one seems to hear,
From the side of the main road
Just about to be plucked up by the gutter.
Cars have tried their way with my body,
Petals clawed by beasts,
All I hear is multiple heartbeats
But I don't have a heart!
A mess, dry and soiled -
All I have to show is my scent;
That flicker of flaring flavour,
My visible persona that could draw women's faces to my bud.
Like a battered virgin,
I have bought no lovers happiness
And I shall spend the rest of my short life
Crushed under mortar shoes.
No clean pots with water,
No humming to help me blossom out,
Such a mistake to grow and be harvested.
My name, rose, does not match my look -
A homeless man's companion.

Beatrice Murphy

WILDERNESS

One more tarnished bauble to hang
On the tree of broken dreams
That stands alone in a wilderness
Of frozen teardrop streams,
Where biting winds of memories
Pound fierce against a grieving heart
Stretching the delicate fabric of hope
Until it tears the soul apart.
Far off on the horizon
Beyond the grim grey meandering plain
Of ash from burned out optimism
That life's cold dagger has slain,
Within the towering fortress
Of her imposing palace of stone,
The Goddess of Misfortune
Holds court from her ivory throne.
Mother of all human misery
Luring with her siren call
All hearts neglected, rejected in love,
Which have been shattered in their fall.
Mistress to the Lord of Despair
Both tugging at the strings of fate,
Forcing the golden shield of hope
To wither in the force of hate.

Bryan Davies

TEARS

Somewhere among these old and cobbled streets,
Where moonshine glistens on the alleyways,
And the sea's soft murmur close at hand,
A single lighted window,
Sends a lonely beacon out across the waves,
To dream of ships far away,
And then a low soft echo sighing on the breeze,
Hush,
Someone's crying in the night.

Paul Hallam

WINNING

Sitting on the plane I try to regain
The appropriate state I should be in
It's not a sin to want to win
But as I stare at the vast outside
Coming last is not an option
My devotion to the task
Is masked by my past failures
Well, all of us are players on a stage called life.
Reading the words off the page
I try to engage I need to comprehend
From start to end when will this lend itself to fulfilment
Contentment.
Or will it lead me to resentment
About the thing I'm meant to be pleased with?
If I just give a smile and file away every conceivable way to stay
Or rather keep at bay my over-excitable, extraordinarily delightable
Feeling off the sheer nearness to winning
As I'm flying above the world I sit curled in my seat
I'm a neat parcel soon be king of my own little castle.

Now walking down the street I'm looking at my feet
Maybe the only way is to cheat
But conceit will surely prelude guilt?
I've built myself a picture in my mind
The only way is to be cruel to be kind
I find it still hard to plan the deceit
I've a small sweat in my hand (that was planned)
But as I aspire toward my goal I perspire
There's no fire just the heat in my head
I'm a liar, or soon to be one
No one sees, suspects or salutes a quiet one
So I can have fun being invisible surely it's understandable
We all want to be noticed, kissed, caressed undressed
And as I journey on my quest I must trust myself to leave others behind
And find my own way of succeeding
Surely it is the winning, people singing your praises
Not just the taking part that stands you apart
And so I won't start but will finish by cheating
Completing it best I would never just feast in my knowledge of how I achieved it
I'm still a little bit doubtful of how I believed it

Eased it into my mind and pushed out the kind
And now all I can find is the need to cheat the joy of conceit
I'm still looking at my feet as I eat the melting sweat
And continue my walk down the street.

Jade Anouka

UNITED

In single file we walk
Herded like cattle along
Blood-soaked muddy pathways
Formed by, neatly attired ranks
Of merciless men
With their pitiless smiles
And ice-capped hearts
Spiting, kicking, punching
Polluted they call us
Not fit to be alive.

We stand huddled together
Against the vile bitterness
Against the callous animosity
That encoils us all
Choking our lungs
Our hands locked together we stand united
Against the oppression that suffocates
The different
Befuddled and groggy
The light slowly fades
As our father comes to welcome us home.

Lee Hart

UNTITLED

If you are offered a drink, take it,
Never mind if it be hemlock;
What better fate than that of Socrates?
Besides, the journey beyond this dimension
Could be the journey of a deathtime:
Who are you to resist going where all
Without exception have gone before
Or are yet to do?
By entering portals of the death-life
One embarks, perhaps, on a great adventure
In uncharted territory. Be that as it may,
Remember to be here now;
The big match between the forces
Of good and evil has already kicked off;
Perhaps you haven't noticed and aren't ready
For your portion of penalties and fouls?
If it makes you feel better, you can appeal
To the referee, by whatever name you call him,
But, remember, your chance to score is over
When the final whistle blows.

Campbell McQueen

THE COUNSELLOR

Trained to read between the lines,
Hear the scream behind the smile,
Exorcise demonic signs, (judging nobody the while).

Crafting, silently, the time,
Ordering each moment's worth;
Unobtrusively sublime,
Noting every pain's rebirth.
Speaking calmly gently firm, ~
Eloquent in quietude;
Listening with deep concern,
Looking no eyes bedewed.
Only sifting grains of light,
Reached from chasms of the night.

Susan Devlin

THE FOUR SEASONS OF MY LIFE

Food. Glorious food!
What would I do without you?
You give hunger the heave-ho
While kissing and caressing
My belly.
Autumn. Glorious autumn!
You knock the spots off the
Summer and its ilk.
The brown, yellow and red leaves dancing and prancing in the air.
The carpeted fronts welcoming you again.
L'armour. Le bon amour!
Vous êtes la vie meme!
La passion de ma vie.
L'aire; la nouritture;
Moon amour; des bisus.

Sleep. Glorious sleep!
The dream of angels kissing me
The flights of escapes while dreaming within a dream
You afford peace, solitude
Joy.

Well, I am what I am.
Je suis.

Kumbi Johnson

SWAN SONG

The swan sang its first sweet note
To the silent stars above:
The snowy bird opened its delicate throat,
The swan sang its first sweet note
The song flew over the castle's moat
Gentle as the touch of the wings of a dove;
The swan sang its first sweet note
To the silent stars above.

Charlotte Meredith

THE RISE AND FALL

In forces of rising human nature
Like once a soldier that mountain climbed
In music your trumpet blowing upwards was true
And in love our height of an arrow reached the peak
In Common Prayer Book of Faith the church steeple touched
In aircraft lights you saw your name lit up
And in conclusion as a civilian you heard from the top of trees
Collar doves whispering, 'You are good'
And seagulls circling and touching the very sexual expression of your face.

In down to Earth curses of troublesome spirits
Like a fish on the bank, a rat trapped in catch
In plagued holy views on this our planet
Where nothing makes sense
And in subway corners you enter the brink of perversion
In the emptiness of an abandoned ship
You sink to the depths with debts
In demolition you crumble like red brick on sod
And in conclusion for whatever rises must fall
And whoever thinks he is beyond will likewise be measured for his coffin!

Simon Boothby

AN ASBO FOR SOME IS NEVER ENOUGH

Clarkson loud music chunders around
Alsatians' barking injuries the sound
Empties of Baileys smash on the ground
An ASBO for some is never enough!

Random expletives yelled for effect
Stealing form family to pay off their debt.
Jeremy Kyle is soon to be met
An ASBO for some is never enough!

You're sent off to Spain to help you calm down
And extra tax credits are given by Brown.
You use them wisely defacing the town.
Two ASBOs for some are never enough!

George Stanworth

AUTUMN'S GOLD

Hedgerows and banks glow with golden tints
Of nut leaf and bracken.
And warm sunlit laced trees lend an invigorating
Combination down shady lanes,
Where colours abound all vying for attention
Of autumn's gold.

Stirring breezes play havoc with the trees -
Sending a colourful array of leaves scattering high and wide -
Dancing willy nilly till they nosedive to the ground,
No longer to enhance
Reduced to shuffling sounds -
When strolling through the mould
Of autumn's gold.

Lifeless trees bereft of colour alas, stand
Dull and tall -
Having shed their coat of many colours -
In the season of the fall,
Of autumn's gold.

Agnes Berry

ETERNITY MOMENT

The scent of May and meadowsweet
loads the air and wafts
to mingle with the song of a thousand birds.
Pale wisteria weeps tears of joy
from age-worn walls of mossy stone
and ancient bright-leaved trees
standing tall through Time's long years
soar their sap to Heaven's arching skies.
And in their dappled shade beneath
a cloud of bluebells quietly glow
reflected in the river's peace.
Here in this ageless steadfast scene
the Kingdom crowds the moment
as centuries meet
in praise.

Helen Seeley

CONQUEST

Cursed are you, my slithering foe
Concealed from my vision
The ancient enmity we share
Has led me to his path of woe
Your calculated deceptions, your insidious treachery
Has masqueraded as the truth
Beguiled by your venomous whisperings
Deluded did I become
Entrapped
Ensnared
Injured I lay
Praying for redemption.

Praise be to you, my constant companion
The manifest reality
Creator of all that was that is, and all that shall be
You are my guiding light
From the abyss of inequity to divine distinction
Your omniscient gaze, your eternal sovereignty
Reigns over me
In winged hope I rise
My spirit soars in your devotion
Cherished
Beloved
Ascending heavenward with adoration.

Aneela Mushtaq

CONTRASTING CORNWALL

A full moon rises over Falmouth Bay;
A huge gold orb that climbs up, up
Into the blue-black sky above
Casting a golden path from sea to shore
Where wavelets ripple on the sandy beach
And all is silent on this summer night.
Perched on the headland, opposite St Mawes,
Pendennis Castle, built by Henry VIII, floodlit
Stands sentinel to watch o'er Carrick Roads
Below, the coastguard station, all alert
For trouble out at sea through day and night,
And ships, lit up, wait out across the bay
To enter port upon the next high tide.
On Cornwall's southern coast this summertime.

Wild winter gales whip up the Atlantic seas.
Great rollers thunder on the shore.
At Perranporth, Godrevy, Fistral Bay,
Black-suited surfers ride the giant waves,
No lifeguards here to guard them as they swim
In cold and treacherous waters on these coasts.
Below the grey and leaden skies above the beach
The seagulls wheel and cry, hunting for fish,
No folks on holiday here to offer food,
No pasties, sandwiches or chips!
The shops are shut; few people walk the streets,
Only the locals live their usual lives
Throughout the winter storms and sunny days
On Cornwall's northern coast this wintertime.

Ann Linney

THE VALE OF BELVOIR

The Vale of Belvoir -
Now there's a place to walk.
No hills to climb, unless you want,
Just walk and talk or stand and look.
Towpaths wending, winding
Following fast the flat waters
Past farms, past villages
Take you where you wish to go.
Bridges framing features
That could be photographs
To hang on walls.
Swans sail up and down
Patrolling their patch.
Sometimes small animals
Cross your path
And water fowl whisk away
Into ripening rushes.
Fishermen silent, seemingly surly
May make a token nod,
One once talked,
Told me of a golden carp.
A fisherman's tale, I thought,
But a hundred yards on,
There he was, near the surface, sunning.
In the late season ripe blackberries abound,
Sweet, juicy, just waiting for the thirsty traveller.
Dragonflies dart then hover 'copter-like
Then dart and dart again.
Towards Langar, trailing from a plane,
You might see black dots appear,
Then like magic they pop into parachutes.
All the bridges are numbered,
Forty five's my favourite.
A tree there sheltered, wild, white violets.
They are gone now, vanished, vandalised.
Today a tea shop pristine isolated,
Welcome where long, dry rambles begin and end,

Waits for walkers and buyers for goods donated
To furnish fund for a nearby hospice.
Parking problems? Not here.
No fee, nor fine to pay, perfect.

R Cooper

JUST A DREAM

Mistiness parting grey greens,
diaphanous wings softly beating
a gentle sound, small, milky
figures flying gently, softly a hair's
breath away from me.

The mists part to reveal
spiky wings, snout noses
and large ears prickly
flights, a menacing sound,
seems frightening to me,
just a hair's breath away.

Soft rustling among the leaves,
bright little eyes and furry
faces snuffling for insects.
A good fairy takes out a
comb and gently grooms the
mouse. Just a hair's breath
away from me.

A robin and a wren
fly down to turn over
the autumn leaves.
I shake some crumbs
out of my pocket. Just
a hair's breath from me.

It's only a dream.

Elizabeth Jenks

COMPULSION

Imbued with frustration and panic, it needs to be done again,
Repulsive compulsion which belies my natural cognitive clarity;
Evangelical purging only exacerbates the pain.

The concept of the matter passing down my eyeline poses questions - am I sane?
My internal justification finds no clear logical parity,
Imbued with frustration and panic, it needs to be done again!

. . .

Calm seas. Control. I embody Vulcan values to the point that I become vain,
Knowledge of the true situation dawns upon my synapse -
Evangelical purging only exacerbates the pain.

Debris! Excreta? With lines of vapour? Body wide itching, eye warmth - bush fire,
Door hands need to be touched, but who touched last - what variety?
Imbued with frustration and panic, it needs to be done again.

Dull refuge, with its *fountain of youth*. Wringing hands and splashing eyes with artificial rain,
Jagged cold sharpness, tiny fissures in my skin, eye bags and discomfort -
Evangelical purging only exacerbates the pain.

I clearly know this is stupid! - This two-dimensional world view that I feign;
But I can't stop dousing, repeating and dousing. An affliction of conscience?
Imbued with frustration and panic, it needs to be done again.

Time departs and the urge dwindles. I contain my mania and retreat to the world,
I walk the halls conversing with minds and joking with colleagues.
Evangelical purging only exacerbates the pain.

Brush hands with someone, not a flutter; dropped books collected from beneath my feet,
I'm coping, ignoring. And the sensation subsides -
Imbued with frustration and panic, it needs to be done again.

I laugh inside, contented and distracted unable to dwell and worry.
Melancholy is far from here; I rejoin the masses and am welcomed.
Evangelical purging only exacerbates the pain.

Far from the end though. If the others leave, or paranoia flares its crest
I'll relapse. I'm tapping my fingers even now. Did I touch the floor?
Brush past a stray-haired coat? Accidentally touch vile baseness? Will I go blind
Or get ill? A disease? Blindness and illness? A vacuum of pathogens? Will I?

Not if . . .

I calmly re-enter my *Fortress of Solitude* where I can become renewed,
The mechanical geysers, the font and my ocular reverence device . . . I was
Imbued with frustration and panic, it needed to be done again
Evangelical purging only *exacerbates* the pain . . . ?

Richard Turner

BEING ALIVE

All I
Can hear is a dog barking and seagulls cry whilst
Washing blows gently backwards and forward in the wind,
Casting its own moving shadow, like a dancing horse on the
Whitened shed door - my accompanying motive,
While I sit in this hot lunch hour on the outdoor step
Triggering childhood memories
Of sitting contentedly on grandparents' steps
Noticing a lawn and border roses, by a quiet road,
And enjoying orange Corona,
Simplicity
While merging naturally with the present,
Like a railway siding meeting the main line.
I notice Lionel cleaning himself and resting in this serene sun spot;
Lying in quiet contentment, a powerful ambience, for current financial thorns,
Reaching to them in silent calm,
Bringing through a message I cannot articulate
Soothing like the softening breeze on my cheeks.
Or the border fern tickling my ear
Yet reaching deeper within me
Becomes the real joy of being alive.

Martin Norman

PANDORA'S BOX

Unique
Elite
Life forms
First breath
Is taken
Blood flows through our veins
Oxygen does its job
The wonder of life
We tread
Through thick and thin
Nature
Nurture
Entwines
Spirit prevails
Cognition at work
This machine
In its day
Lives through life
Environment enfolds
This wonderful specimen
That grasps the light
Ups and downs
We do fare
Strive for life
We do share
As we flourish
The flower
Has opened
World is oyster
Souls
Shall meet
Love conquers
Tremors in life
We endure
Obstacles
Makes us strive
We look
At the stars
The wonder
Of this planet
See its treasures

It unfolds
We are one
As we grow.

Our purpose
To live our lives
Bring offspring into this world
We cherish
We love
Generation
Is spurned
It grows and grows
Nature turns
Family
Friends
Leave our world
The light
Slowly goes down
Out
Their function
Is nil
They take
Knowledge
Guidance
Love
To a wonderful place
In this space
Souls
Forever
They will not be forgotten
Never, never
This Earth
This paradox world
Will turn and turn
The secrets
Will stay
Box of wonder
Another day.

Helen Vesey

POPPIES

How could we know how much we would miss
You? Scarlet paper kites,
Black-seeded hearts of dreamy sleep,
Red flood of Adonis' blood
Pouring unquenchably, richly deep.

You arrogant common weed!
Now no more despised, but longed for.

A single bloom shrivels in scorching glare.
A small rebel flag, defiantly dares
To wave from baked soil, blackened grass,
Where once docile lizards now claw and scrap.

A car, heedless of your imminent doom,
Slices through, drowning your small insurrection
In spirals of sickening, choking grey spume.
And, heartsore at your final destruction,
We yearn for showers of sweet, cleansing rain,
And fields awash with poppies again.

Margaret Gill

UNTITLED

My life itches at this early morning hour
Scratching, I ponder with whose fleas
I have lain down and out, as round I go.
I shall make myself a coffee now
To soothe away the sad, bad melodies
Of stale breath.

My toothpaste has betrayed me
I shall use my razor to shave away my mind.

Laurence H Sullivan

THE DREAM

I looked down, and the concrete,
Bare and grey and cold, looked back up at me.
And it stretched way into the distance,
Mile upon mile of greyness.
Cars pumped out toxic fumes as they drove
Bumper to bumper on the eternal grey roads.
Frazzled, hassled drivers got irritable again,
It's rush hour.

I looked up, and the shiny glass shone back at me,
Strange shapes have appeared on the skyline,
Stretching up, ever thinner and higher.
And people sit at rows and rows of desks,
And tap, tap, tap away on their keyboards,
Answering ever more emails and 'staying in touch'
They stretch, and complain of repetitive strain injury,
What is that about?

We go home to our centrally heated hot houses,
Ever burning up oil and gas supplies,
And cook our oven ready meals in a microwave.
Rarely do we stop and look,
Rarely do we have time to 'just be'.
The clock ticks on, our lives are in fast forward.

Where is this England? This green and pleasant land . . .
I take a trip; I struggle to get there,
To where the air is fresh, the stars are bright,
The sun warming the rich dark earth
And the farmer toils to grow earthy foods
And cattle graze once more.
I wake, the clock tells me it's all too late . . .

Jane Wade

HE STANDS WHERE ALL HIS MARTYRS LIE

The Valetta Caravaggio outshone
All other splendours in the Co-Cathedral
Of St John where Baptist's head
Extended before the blade in very act of horror
And of dread. Such glowing light
From such an awe-filled sight; the painted, indifferent cluster witnessing
Eternally the act; the tourists in the oratory briefly viewing in their
Hurried Maltese pilgrimage.

I leaned against the wall and heard them leave.
My eyes were captivated by the pool,
The crimson blood pool spreading on the dungeon floor,
Once more a memory of time suppressed
Distressed my eyes. Shiraz. Iran. An early revolution death.
Our priest and friend. Another floor. Another blade.
Another pool of crimson spreading. Another close-up
Cause for dreading.
Another group of witnesses; these were men
Who might be next, all law suspended,
All tolerance for Christian service ended beyond immediate
Resuscitation.

Guide me into peace, my friend, in prayer.
How can the church's seed-time bear the necessary pain?
'Remember in the lifelong image in your mind
The ever-present Christ.' I find and see Him standing there
In splendour beyond painting, where all His martyrs lie.
I see Him now. I see Him there and here
And hear His voice commanding, 'Peace, be still.'

Christopher Payne

A MOTHER'S VIEW FROM THE CLIFFS

(Written with empathy and dedicated to the parents and carers of drug and alcohol abusers)

The sky merges with the sea
All I remember is you and me
The way it was what it became
How things will never be the same.

The clouds hang heavy in the steely sky
The ghastly truth revealed, why, oh why?
Chasing the dragon, slithering like quicksilver
Heroin, the killer.

Pale and gaunt, with features drawn
Can I recognise my child, my son?
Will he succumb, will he drift away
Or will he live to fight another day?

I need to know he understands
How the family, ravaged at his hands
Feel the sense of loss, their aching hearts
Puzzled by his indifference, standing apart.

The mighty killer runs through his veins
Destroys his life, enslaves his brain
Allows no sense of wrong and right
The pleasure sustains him into the night.

As I stand looking out to sea
All I still remember is you and me
The child who ran along the sand
The mum who took him by the hand.

It would appear the scene is set
Bewildered, no solutions yet
I want to hope, I pray to see
The best, my son, of you and me.

Barbara Blyth

A HISTORY OF DANCING

I am the boy in the stiff white shirt,
sticky-footed on the edge of the hall,
waiting for the song to stop
or the eye contact to begin,
whichever is the sooner.

I am the smiler in the white T-shirt,
surrounded by his whistle posse,
wild in warehouses, happy and hardcore,
sweating off the rubdown
and coming up up up.

I am the swayer with the white eyes,
charging from shoulder to shoulder
and embrace,
unsteady in steady rhythm,
lurching through another fandango.

I am the white statue
blissed out under ultraviolet light,
303 squelching into me,
bassline sneaking round my kidneys,
as I shudder into ecstasy.

I am the guy on the white sand,
feet anchored as the beat flows to the sea,
and we roll our bodies one more time
and salute the sun
as the melody rises.

I am the whisper in the white jeans,
slicksharp and seen on the scene,
leading the cheers from behind the golden rope
as rapture banishes the Hudson blues ~
and a DJ saves my life.

I am the elegance in the white tails,
swinging Ginger with clockwork precision
around a champagne flute
or, Moses supposes, I'm running up a sofa
to kiss Debbie good morning.

I am the patron in front of the white lights,
observing, noting, delighting
in talking without words,
of shapes thrown and stories told
by limbs' liminal curves.

I am the shuffler on the white carpet,
headphones a passport to a recombinant world;
music might sound better with you,
but it's only on the dance floor
that I'm a superstar, that I am free.

I am the star in the white suit,
all pace and poise, grace and glide
in the guise of the romantic hero;
finger locked in, eyes ablaze;
electric steps lead to electricity when we leave.

I am the man with the white hair,
waiting now on one more waltz;
gentle twirls spark giddy memories
across the card. I'm glad I cut in;
and I'm glad I asked you.

Rishi Dastidar

BUTTERFLIES

Painted mysteries appear startled by
the water's reflection,
closely followed by blushing red cheeks
as brush painted coloured tears fall,
like green encrusted emerald jewels which
settle gently upon ruby red petals,
of thorn stemmed wild flower roses
and sunlight spirals reflect warmth
from their placid golden halos,
as the mockingbird's chorus echoes sweetly
o'er the sound of clear rippling waters.

Alec Skelson

THE APPOINTMENT

How often have I contemplated
being here rehearsing speeches and subtle reasoning!
Standing still in slanting shadows
by concrete stairs,
in this dim coldness
like winter held within glass and brick,
beneath wall lights plucked out or never placed
like bloodless eye sockets.

These stairs have a mockery of their own
in each dallying thought,
in languishing over what is going further away.
There is no compassion here
in this reluctant passage to the final barrier.

I raise my fist
and sense him within shifting books and papers,
marshalling his denials and excuses
preserving an old order.

My knocking reverberates.
His voice is drowned in cacophonous sound.

Seconds stretch.

The door is flung wide.
Light flares from a window.
Then all is silent
suddenly
as a switch thrown.

He stands in shadow.
I sit as one undergoing interrogation stammering out explanations,
trying to bring reason into that which cannot reason
but only knows its essence.
My pleas are impassioned.
Yet he remains pale - the controller of fates,
speaking of a friendship,
exonerating another of the blame that I apportion.

The room becomes stifling.
Paper gives off its print odours in chaos of heat.
I blurt out the truth
against indifference
through altercations

offering myself,
but he will not accept substitutes
and his apologies are unwarranted even though desired.

I leave and close the door.

This aura,
this place,
all concentration and sharpness once his
are compelled to fade to background,
and a void exists where non-recovery seems eternal.

He hears the sound of retreating footsteps,
and a door slams on a world that could not be broken into by default
with its times of waiting in corridors
and by forbidden portals.
Beneath his window
laburnum blossom
falls deadly in its beauty.
He looks on.
Heat burns through black.
And another is pleased at someone gone.
Begun by accident,
finished by intent,
I run,
he sees me fall.

Christine Ann Moore

HIDDEN HISTORIES

I passed through forgotten locations,
Forgotten weeks ago,
off tracks deserted with a mine shaft hidden,
no warning notice of the hole
if only I had known that
it was a warning from my past,
a place laid deep
down in my psyche - best forgot,
some recollect with fondness,
not me - best forgot!

Carole Smith

FOND FAREWELL

They are a dying breed.

No more their music
fills the air,
nor bursts of laugher
echo down
their corridors of time.

No more the wood
that's scarred with
countless years
of people's pleasure,
or carpets soaked
with alcohol (or blood).

No more the ever
ready ear to lift us up
when we are down
or cheer with us
when we are up,
nor harbour many
secrets as they
seep into the wall.

No more attended
by the mass
that often spent
as much as they could
and sometimes
even more.

They are a dying breed.

Now devoid
of human life,
a lone façade
of tags
and boarded windows,
where pigeons
desecrate the walls
and claim the halls
as theirs.

Mournful requiem
silenced forever
lamenting loss
where people tread no more
nor channel
recollections to the ether.

We raise no glass
and bid farewell
through sober tears
just say goodbye forever to:

The Propeller
The Black Horse
The Leslie Arms
The Red Lion
The Half Moon
The King's Arms
The Star of India

May their *spirits*
Rest in peace.

Jillian Henderson-Long

A NATURALIST'S PRAYER AT BEDTIME

The light lifts
the falling dust

as it falls like snow
the fluffy kind

not much caring for gravity
specks sailing on air

I breathe down
they sail up

I watch
they are silent . . .

I switch out the lamp
my settled mind sleeps.

Ray Jackie Dowling

UNCHARTED DEPTHS

Actually, Granny,
It was me, all the time;
playing the innocent,
cheeks blazing.

Yes, I was lying. Fancy that.
'Goodness dear,' I hear you saying, 'I wonder how
you could have been so thoughtless.'

That important lesson
you were seeking to impart, so long ago:
conveyed not by a good quick slap,
but conscientious coals of fire,
with which, for my trouble, I was liberally singed,
as you strained to fathom
a grandchild's waywardness.

Still smouldering after all these years,
I can tell you now, Granny:
the bottom isn't where you thought it was.
Who knows: maybe there isn't one . . .

Andrew Greaves

TIME

Lost in the wilderness
You see no echo
The wilderness same as darkness
Has no foreseeable end
Everyone planning busy, busy
Who knows what will unfold
If anything

What is the point of searching, searching
Because what you are searching for
Is not there
Only in your heart?
Everyone passes by
In a hurry, hurry
Why is this time the essence?

May Wood

134

THE SECRET SELF

There is a place within our mind,
Where hopes and dreams lie scattered and concealed.
Fear, fantasy, love and longings there roam free,
A veiled and hidden shrine therein, locked away with a key.

What others will never see or know,
Remain forever the shrouded images of our psyche.
The secrets, promises and inner thoughts which we hide,
Are contained and nurtured here, where our strongest feelings reside.

One's true disposition then, can never be entirely understood,
Since the essence of individuality shall forever remain elusive.
Thoughts on people and life we may never fully reveal,
Should our face adopt a mask to disguise what we really feel!

Behind our everyday persona lies a myriad of expectations,
Where on a flight of fancy we can envisage changing our lives.
People place us in little boxes to make the picture whole,
But there is invariably a distortion, if we could see into the soul.

The core of our basic nature is often a painful place to visit,
Seeing as it contains both the better and worse parts of ourselves.
A centre of emotion which records our anguish and our pleasures,
Sadness and happiness dwelling side by side in equal measures.

And while we cry here, we may outwardly laugh along with the world,
Or when we are successful, we cloak the fear this brings here.
What, through chance or fate, should a new day choose to reveal,
Through reason and understanding only we can nourish or heal.

Selective memories from childhood to adulthood abide here like ghosts,
Episodes and chapters, their subject matter sometimes clear, sometimes
blurred.
Those who are special, loved, or lost, in this place we can find,
Beautiful recollections remain pure in this part of our mind.

All past and future wishes reside in our inner self,
So in our lifetime, let us be so inspired to see them come true.
What is painful should be forgotten, while laughter should thrive.
Let our mind be a flourishing garden with the rotten dead, the good alive!

Mary Carroll

DESERT

So proud I am to stand this tall -
Asbestos floors
Are creaking more.
And so brave I feel to lick the flame -
Soft foolish tongues
Are just among
The rags we cast to warm our hands,
The fuel to smoke out our demands,
Or hopes, of fears, or simply words
To catch connection by the way of birds.

O' so humble am I in tent, on trek,
But bowing heads
Leaves showing neck.
So graced I feel to stare at feet -
My bowing head
Begs guillotine.

By these barren lands and my wind-beat back,
By throbbing calves and stinging hands,
By my valour, of which I stole,
By heart, by strength, and by my soul
I announce struggle's resting place,
Sprinkled with sweat off of my dirtied face,
Be a hole by an oasis
Where I will loosen my laces,
And breathe without taking paces,
Before burying the body
In the moist sand.
So proud I am, so tall I stand.

So whole I feel with sights like these,
So precious plains, so luscious trees.
So content I am as I stare beyond -
So hungry it is as it leers at me.

Benjamin Hamilton

LILAC BLOSSOMS

Pendulous, plump lilac blossoms
heavily laden on the bough
perfuming the air with their
sublime, heady presence,
assailing our senses, long ere we
chanced upon this stunning scene.

Resembling half-furled summer parasols
these bounteous blooms, fair tumbling down
with gentle, heart-shaped pale green leaves,
swaying lightly, framing such a rambling
picture of beauty - overhanging
a dry-stone walled, country garden.

Heart-stopping and yet, calming,
God must have been out early
with His celestial painting palette
to so delight our eyes on encountering
this sublime scene - laid out to beckon us forth
and in so doing, to captivate our hearts.

Gloria Jean Cambell

SARA KHAWAD

What rolling hate commands you?
Which trembling breath of quiet envy
Curdled hot inside your throat?
And those who crawl behind you
Scratched their way up from beneath the Earth.
The bullet! The brain!
Insane . . .
A name
A name
A name
A name.
A child's smile, a mother's shame.
The cradles never fell -
You piled them all in front of speeding trains.

James Burt

REMEMBER?

How can I say, 'remember me' when I do not yet exist?
But if you care for history, care for me, its reverse:
Years, decades, centuries, millennia waiting to happen,
Much of what I might or will be dependent on you.

You revere your past ages, combing the soil, meticulously
Seeking all signs of ancestors - grains of food, chips of flint -
Whilst for my searching you leave great plastic mountains
And countless records of what is or used to be.
Often the history you know is pretty: fine clothes and noble deeds,
Stories of those more memorable people whose names live on.
More logically you mourn your war dead - too many to name -
Sad drawing-down of blinds for flesh pitted against machines.
Rarely you acknowledge time-distant sufferers of plague and tyranny,
The countless masses that lived in centuries of fear and superstition,
Surviving wretchedly, leeched by the rich and powerful,
Their children dying more often than they lived.

This present (not forever) age seems kinder now to all humanity.
Even your weapons claim intelligence to dodge the innocent.
You weep for suffering, yearn to help, support kindly charities.
You affirm the right of each individual to freedom and happiness.
Seeing in each an inner light that must never wilfully be put out,
You devise amazing cures, heal the sick, support the weak.
You protect the rights of all and count as beneficial most quests for wealth.
Pursuing their dreams, each generation grows richer that the last.
But as comfort grows you empty your seas, your mines, your forests,
Your many children multiplying from millions into billions.
Do you think without true thought the horrors of the past are gone forever?
That progress always means improvement, more benevolence?

Remember me - the longer part of history that is still to come!
As you grieve for the sorrows of a past that cannot change,
Don't neglect a future that transforms by what you do:
Leave me a world as beautiful as yours.

Christine Sanderson

PERIPHERY

On the perimeter, the outside edge,
Standing in the cool shadows,
Never within the warm ambit
    Of the inner circle.

Observing the group interacting together,
Body language, laugher, conversation,
The 'in' jokes, all happy as one
    Sharing a common bond.

Then you see tensions insidiously creep in,
Like a snake slithering through the grass.
The glib rejoinders masking a cruel,
    Subtle mockery.

Complacency suffuses your whole being,
As you welcome the outer circle's security,
Its carapace shielding you from the pitfalls
    Of the inner circle.

Fragile social structures crumble.
The inner circle replaces the outer,
The watcher becomes the watched,
    A reversal of the status quo.

The brittle laughter of the social set
    Fades to a distant echo
        Dying in the wind.

Alison Drever

FAR FROM THE MEADOW

Cut grass sweet, summer-scented, soothing, green,
Stirs inklings of a fierce primal past
Rooted beneath a pleasant garden scene . . .
Mow the lawn retired man,
Taming the grass that civilised you,
Far, far from the meadow where
Shoulder-high the wild grasses grew,
Wheat-eared, barley-whispered, rye-sharp and rough,
Thrusting up, broad, coarse and strong,
Blade after blade, tangled and tough;
Far, far from your forebear crouched for the kill,
His heart cold as the sharp stone in his hand,
Necessity keeping him rigid and still,
Closing his mind to everything but
His immediate need of something to eat.
Didn't see beauty, didn't feel pity
For the wild creature bleeding at his feet.
Didn't notice the meadow's varied yield,
Quivering seed heads, fronded, shiny, smooth;
No vision of bread from a golden field,
A settled life and time to think and be;
His hunting ground a sunlit picnic place
Where people could sit contemplatively.
Ages and Ages of Stone would pass
Before his descendants discovered the secrets of grass.
Centuries, millennia between
The man with the mower
And him.

Pam Hatcher

ENGLAND AND ST GEORGE

I have but one thing in my mind
A passion burning bright
Crossed be my heart a fiery red
On a field of the purest white.

The light shall not fade on England now
The fields be forever green
The character charm that is England now
In my heart means everything.

The rising sun on the sleepy hills
The twinkle of morning dew
The running stream to the rivers flow
And on to the sea of blue.

The light shall not fade within my eyes
Nor stifle my mind within
My ears will not want whilst still the sound
Of the song that the blackbird sings.

The light shall not fade on castle walls
Nor the heroic deeds of Man
The bells will forever ring so clear
In the churches of our land.

The light shall not fade whilst vigil be
The eye of Heaven bright
For our cause be true and our loyalty be
In trust with our red crossed knight.

The light shall not fade on England now
The fields be forever green
The character, charm that is England now
In my heart means everything.

Maxwell Dunlop

PROMISE

The final music from the church organ drifted across
As I sat on the corner of the tombstone
And pondered life.
It all seems so fast and complicated,
So much to do,
So little time in which to do it,
So many choices and decisions.

Constantly bombarded by
'Buy this', 'Enrol on that'
By so doing we will be
Healthier, wealthier,
Slimmer, happier,
Fulfilled, contented,
And have an army of friends
Who are as successful at it
As we are.

It's so bewildering
That I don't know which way to turn.
So many choices,
So little time.
Was it like that for the incumbents of my seat?
Now just bones and dust
In the corner of a forgotten time,
What was it like for them?
Long forgotten - out of sight, out of mind,
Yet they had their joys and sorrows,
Just like me.
Perhaps it was simpler then,
Fewer choices,
But maybe starker ones.

Maybe it is time to stop,
To shut out the cacophony of the urgent
And to figure out
Just what is important,
And do it.

Then, perhaps
I will fulfil that promise of the life
I have been entrusted with.
Just like them.

Georgina Wilson

SECRET REALMS

Shadows guard the entrance to our secret realms
Guarding all the mysteries that fantasy overwhelms.

A sanctuary of privacy riddled with one's belief
Adorned by every moment in solitude and peace.

We traverse the moment, a world our freedom stole
Walking beyond the labyrinths trapped within our soul.

In these sacred catacombs darkness turns to light
Reality is abandoned and dreams turn into life.

Memories become a treasure we harvest on this land
Pastures filled with secrecy there at our command.

We cultivate our freedom let our dreams run wild
Dodging all responsibility just like a cunning child.

Imagination is our genie granting us this bliss
Everything we ever want lives within its wish.

As the sole dictator, keeper of every dream
Ruler of the dynasty of our own regime.

This secret realm invites us to our own eternity
We occupy its odyssey whenever we are free.

Just for a moment we walk its sacred shore
If reality tries to enter, shadows close the door.

David Bridgewater

DROWNING

Lost in the ocean with the forever changing tide,
carried by the waves of time.
The blue swirling myth of the siren echoes in the depths,
as my eyes open wide one final time.
My mind whirls with curiosity as the beauty of the ocean welcomes me,
this is my new home and I'm filled with uncertainty,
the swirling of the water so calm and gentle.
I'd like to say silence is heard
but the ocean is a busy place
filled with music of hers.
It sings to me,
the beauty I hear it, it enchants me.
Notes so soft and gentle lure me to the doom of my sea-bed temple.
I see her but she's like no other,
not a boat, for she has no rudder.
A woman I see standing there,
covered in scales with an evil glare.
She's as green as grass with a piercing stare,
she twinkles like a star from way up there.
Don't underestimate this vision of purity,
as she dwells in the blue depths of the ocean with an evil red gaze.
This lady commits her perilous crime,
without an ounce of sorrow to those who are sublime.
My body hits the ocean floor
my soft seabed of sand buries me more,
the shells on the floor flicker in the light like candles.
The harlequin jellyfish transmit light like those of stained glass,
the dark of the ocean makes a fine coffin
the coral reefs fill with strange creatures they're my only friends here,
coming to say goodbye, one final time.
And there she stands proudly glistening in her own glory
as she closes the final chapter of your story,
claiming your life,
now you're the star of her murder story.

Sally Butler

IMPRINTS

The crumbling house
has been visited many times
since that life disappeared
into fettered memories,
the cracked pathway
and neglected garden
dry with the dust of pollution.

Little fingerprints remain
haunting each room
with coloured images,
and by the back door
a faded growth chart,
inches pencilled in with pride.

Leaves rustle and fly
outside the cold window
while a small pair of red boots,
left behind in the rush to leave,
stand cobwebbed to the floor.

Rachel Treadwell

THE LOVE LAUNDRY

I washed my bed sheets today
(It's three weeks since you left.)
I sat and watched them spin for a
bit and regret washed over me.
I had robbed them.
(I had robbed myself)
of your smell
of your stain,
of the faint trace that remained of
your brief love for me.
Just like all those times I showered in
the mornings after we had made love.

Emma O'Mahony

NOCTURNE

Darkness rolls towards me, hiding
corners, culverts curves. Headlights burn
black billows of time. Travellers
pass from behind in swirls of light,
disappear into night's menace.

Engine hums. Steadying music
fills the void, calming and soothing
as I steer through Stygian gloom.

Far in the distance lights approach:
prowling jungle animals hunt
the night for prey. Cautious, I keep
well to the side, leave wide margins
for their manoeuvres, their errors.

The road sweeps down out of the pass.
Tension eases. I breathe deeply
and head for home.

Joan Lees

FROM A DAUGHTER

I often think of you
quite suddenly in brief cameos,
vivid images, which focus, fade,
then reappear.
A smile on the edge of laugher,
your gaze held in conversation,
a favourite scent drifting on a draught of air.
Small fragments of your wholeness,
held for fleeting moments,
made real by the intensity
of my longing.
I often think of our goodbye,
wishing it had been an embrace,
instead of the hurried kiss
in flight between us.

Helen Clarke

ROCK

Dear rock,
I am shocked to see you so dead.
Lets talk
My grandmother says, that the rocks have an ability to hear . . .
Can you hear me? Dear rock?
I have a confession to make . . .
'I hate you' . . .
With your rockyness,
Your extreme sharpness,
Your insensitiveness . . .
You are pre-occupied with your ego,
All the time
And you have no time to respond back!
Why were you born at all,
When you had to live like a dead!
Emotionless . . .
Love comes to caress you
With a perfumed zephyr;
Either you are dumb
Or you just don't care . . .
Love comes to lick you
In form of drops of rain;
But you become dry in a moment
Each time you refrain.
Love comes to see you
In form of the sun rays;
It tries hard to penetrate
But never does a flower grow.
Years go by
And you are still there,
Unchanged
Unaware
Missing the goal of living
Missing, enjoying . . .
I pity you . . .

Dear rock,
I have one more confession to make,
You are the best listener,
I have ever met . . .

Priya Shah

EPIPHANY OVER DINNER

Mother (yours) exacts her influence, her pull
on the boy who stayed and tried to pretend a family.
I see her looking, glancing, judging:
would this be the girl for you?
I was later to bear that look
turned to pity, incomprehension.
How could I stand you
when you had nothing for me?

You
offered nothing, yet everything;
that she didn't know
as she dished out Sunday dinner and veiled disapproval.
All nods smiles polite chit chat,
the old tea and sympathy for me.
Politeness, courtesy
like serving up another course for me,
came so effortlessly to both of you.

Me
with my roots in Pennine soil
steeped in loss (similar yet different from yours)
couldn't do 'restrained', 'polite'
Instead I yelled, shouted, demanded
after another meal.
This time, with you and an absent father,
so obliviously your father it broke my heart.
You thirty years on
with every ounce of your ancestral charm
and danger in the battle of Great Wall of China,
Chinese banquet and absent mistress.

I was as assaulted by his charm
as yours
That is until I remembered Durham School:
your brother shutting himself away,
the absent mistress and absent mother
and I saw you through this family's glass.

A different reflection from the one I had known
and howled again for loss of you.
For in a moment of alcohol-fuelled clarity.
I saw nothing could pull down the great walls of China
you had built.

Joanne Potts

BLACKBIRD

Gargled trill, cut grass fresh,
Recounts the day with full puffed breast.
From upright hedge so stiff and gnarled,
The hidden voice of eventide.
Rounded, twisted, tangled warble,
Gently laments the sinking ball.
Perfect structure, perfect time,
Restful excitement, tight entwined.
Swallowed and gulped through throaty gasp,
Abstract sonnet out of grasp.
Sweet and delicate, fragile notes,
Awakens peace and warms our hope.
Romantic tongue, a babbling stream,
O'er pebbles of emotion, through twists of green.
A tranquil brook of crystal swells,
A shallow path through vocal bells.
Without words, a familiar song,
We hear no begin, but then it's gone,
As limp skies empty. Foxes bicker,
Silence falls as lane lights flicker.

Vincent Ryan

NO PLACE TO HIDE

Dull and dark, unsettled weather,
rain and hail, a touch of snow,
gale force winds, a hurricane threatens,
no mercy when a cyclone blows.
Through the night the wind increased,
spiralling inwards as the pressure grew.
A violent storm - a hurricane,
all at sea now in danger,
no place to hide from whence it came.
Gale force winds hit the coastline,
travelling north in a shift of wind,
early morning the storm engulfed,
no one aware what was destined.
Disaster struck outside the harbour,
boats in danger all around,
pilot boats that could not lead,
their paths unable to be found.
Distress signals, flares galore
vanished in the night-time air,
swallowed up by a storm of darkness,
with helpless feelings everywhere.
That night there were many wrecks
the 'Royal Charter' the biggest yet.
The greatest tragedy ever, in peacetime not in war,
four hundred and fifty lives were lost, the biggest loss by far.
Just yards from safety, the storm caused such a plight,
men, women and children snatched from their beds in the black of night.
The wreck that shocked a nation,
no hope of rescue or salvation.
The 'Iron Ship,' a large steam clipper,
tossed at sea like a velvet slipper.
Three thirty early morning, on the face of the vessel's clock,
when the ill-fated ship was tossed and thrown against the jagged rock.
The 'Royal Charter' was its name,
lost, destroyed, a storm to blame.
Families returning home, with their hard-earned wealth,
fruits of their labour, honest work, no underhanded stealth.
Ingots of gold down in the hold, money belts filled with nuggets,
around their waists and in their pockets,
riches from where they had dug it.
A rough and rocky journey home,

fatal endings in a storm.
Only forty men survived that night
when the clipper ship plunged out of sight.
Hitting the rocks and splitting in two,
when cyclonic winds battered and blew.

Audrey Taylor

WINTER

In a bold black sky
lying cradled low,
a virgin moon
silently, stares back.

Diamonds play in
patterned array,
illuminate the waiting
watcher's way.

On the earth's
brown throw,
green on green,
spiky spears
slash and scar.
Bobbled heads alight
give show.
Crocus, Snowdrop and
Winter Aconite.

Stoney houses in shadowed sleep,
drapes drawn against the night.
From frosted panes
glows of warm light,
softly, gently, peep.

Judy Hallas

SMILING EYES

Flawless beauty,
A luscious rose.

Admired from afar,
By some with glances of jealousy.

A porcelain doll,
Perfect and pristine.

But no one close enough
To see the cracks beneath her skin.

She smiles to the world,
Her glittering gleam.

But no one sees
How it wavers and falls
When she is alone.

Unattainable, not worth the risk,
Some say too perfect,
Too far a height to fall.

If they look close enough
Maybe they'll see her flaws
The mask behind her smiling eyes.

For she is far from perfect,
Fragile beneath the surface.

Timeless beauty she may appear,
But tragically beautiful is what she is.

She lies through her eyes
About the agony inside,
Look once again
And see hope drowning in the pools of darkness.

Her heart is surrounded by emptiness,
A hollow shell remains
Her soul dwindles away.

She is to be admired but never to be touched,
An unopened book,
Her spine holds richness
Filled with character
But no one to read her story.

She waits,
But fears no one is coming
To rekindle her soul,

To rescue her from the darkness
Into which she falls.

No one to heal her scars
Or make her heart flutter.

She waits,
Flawless but full of flaws.

The surface cracks deepen
Until the stars in her eyes
Begin to fade away.

She waits.

Aqeelah Yusuf

UPLOADERS

The Dorset hill stands high above
Solid in the early morning sun
Whose prying light casts contoured shadows
Across strip lynchetts marking man's
Ancient hard won strips of soil.

Cattle now graze where crops once grew
But still walk down the road at milking time,
The road where lengthmen broke the stone
And cut the ditch by the narrow bridge
They built with graceful arches replacing the ford.

The stream runs deep past lichened apple trees
And echoes on past oak and willow,
Flowers and ferns which line the banks
Until an open pool of sunlight
Dapples down onto a speckling trout.

The sun is higher now and in the shimmering heat
The towering oaks seem near the sky
Where a lone buzzard thermals slowly
With piercing gaze seeking a hapless rabbit
Midway between the sea and Eggardon Hill.

David Tas

THE SILENT WATCHERS WAIT

Among the dark valleys of the world
All through the day and night
Through mists and shadows and veils entwirled
The silent watchers wait - and look for light
As each great star twinkles and scintillates
In the vastness of the firmament
So each human spirit twinkles and scintillates the brighter
With every noble thought
And even brighter still as each noble thought is activated
And absorbed into the life pattern of the thinker.

This is the light they seek, those silent watchers who wait and
As the light of the spirit glows brighter
With every noble thought and deed
So this glowing spark flickers and flashes like the dazzling glitter
Across the rippling surface of a lake in full sunshine
Attracting the attention of those watchers.

Then from the lofty plateaus where wisdom and enlightenment
Are the bread and water of life
Comes down that responding flash of inspiration which emblazons
Our own dim glimmer
Into a radiant reflection of pure divine light.

'Tis written
'The spirit of Man is as the lamp of God
Wherewith He searcheth the inwardness of all secrets.'
So - is your lamp lit? - then let your light shine
With love of all that is good and true
Fan the flame of your spiritual desire
So that it may burn the brighter
Trim the wick with the knowledge, wisdom and enlightenment
Gained from life's experiences,
Fill the bowl with the oil of human kindness and brotherly love,
Keep noble your thoughts and nobler your deeds and
Let there be light - more light - your light.

Walter Thomas Soilleux

THE NATURAL MAGIC RANGE

For those who crave a subtle touch can we
suggest our perfume 'Essence of the Fall.' In
glass the amber of a lion's eye we draw on
fading warmth in tones of russet earth and
wood smoke, apple crisp and blackberry with
juices from the vine. This wistful and alluring
scent evokes a memory of gently drifting leaves.

For those in search of mystery, the enigmatic
rare today in all its habitats we recommend our
face and body lotion. Silver drops and moon cream
blend with tincture of a leopard, undulating, silent,
velvet smooth. Order more than one and we'll
include completely free of charge a question mark
available in shades of wild cerise and purple haze.

For those in need of inspiration why not try our
'Glitter' bathtime mix of stars and sparks. One
cupful under running water stimulates the vision
and restores your fading dreams to life. Turn off
the working world, turn on the dark and as your
aspirations soar again experience a firework touched
by heaven. Wish control included. Use with care.

For all the SAD who lean into their boxes waiting
for the voice of spring, a summer's touch through
ultraviolet we have eye drops made with natural
sunlight. Dawn fresh quality with anti-glare. Or
why not try our powdered candle flame, a top
bestselling mix of radiance, tranquillity and hope.
Stir in tea or coffee for that deeper glow inside.

For all the people everywhere
whose souls are bruised and grey
our healing balm is recommended.
Daily application as required.

Nicola Wood

WELSH POET BLASPHEMY

Being and nothingness
Nothingness and being
Poet destroys.

Love's stars
Black night skies
Absinthe lust
Primitive pagan words
Whisper, 'God is dead'

Lobsters chase Jean Paul
Down the Champs Elysée
Plan a 'Fleurs des Mal'

Elders in the chapel
Boneless frauds
Drive Idris to play ball
Kinnocks get Barons
Welsh Secretary Joes
Play musical chairs
Welsh assembly
Hay on way
Trip to Dante
Seventh circle of Hell
Welsh mercenaries
International brigades
Hit Quaeda
Dien bien Phu
Incommensurability Good Friday.

Paul Faulkner

SEASONS

Silent phantoms with intriguing times
As we look on with bated breath
Your seasons are changing
With reasons only you can't explain
With words only actions.

They are muddled and troubled
Humanity awaits helplessly
For what was their norm
Is being revalued.

Like the change in Man
As he ages
As his spine crumbles

Is this you my Mother Earth?
Has your spine aged?
Has it been your decision
To end what Man has known?
Has it been Man who's made you decide?

You have changed before many times
And risen like a phoenix
From the ashes.
And Man awaits the change
Wondering, will they rise too?

Sandra Miles

STRANGE SKIN

There is this skin
That is not
The skin of a stranger.
Yet it is a strange skin
That can hold her
On a frozen path of fear
And torment her so closely.
She is no more her own
There is this voice
Such a well-known voice
And she knows it should not be there.

'Salty vinegar,' the voice says
'Sweet salty vinegar'
'Do you truly care?' he asks
And turns the key tightly
On the cell door he is closing in her soul
Smiling, he swears her to secrecy
While she falls in his darkness,
A red soul tear.

There is this game
She is playing
Learning the golden rule
Silence . . .
De-rooted,
Looking inward for her own
Latch key.
All night smiling
Disco dancing,
No one will know
No one will understand
She'll be her own ghost
In her own safety zone
Inside herself, alone

And who is going to show her
After all those lone years
The gentle power of tenderness
When trust only brought her
Tears
And pain
In his cage.

M Lahrem

ANON

Oh to draw that lucky hand
That has dealt so few of late
And play forth with triumphant band
On the heels of some steadied fate

To bate the breath of hate and curse
And pass that jagged edge to thee
Who know not of better, nor of worse
Who lay as dead in apathy

Yet to you I cling, as frenzied lover
To your shielded stomach of lead
I banish my demons to aggrieve another
So let rest this wearied head

For pray I wish not to understand
Here I pray for wit that's slow
Then I could join your married band
Who see only as you know

So tip me that ignorant
Sensationalist currency
For I am out of pocket, all is spent
And I have not love in this poverty.

Georgia Rushton-Read

RAINBOW

High in the sky
When it rains and it is sunny
There are rainbows.
From the firmament they arch
Hover into Heaven and descend into Earth
A rainbow of colours
Sun's rays in falling rain.
An iridescence of colours
Forming itself into a rainbow of hope.
Lips smiling, it has strength
And chooses its own Electra of power
A new beginning, a genesis of new growth
The rainbow of my love, of God's love
And my heart, too, leapt with joy
As my eye saw Iris in descent.

I'd been watching the rain
drenched inside
Trying to forget I'd seen the sun
go down
And I was crying psychedelic tears
A kaleidoscope of turmoil
But rain or sunshine didn't matter
I could see the rainbow
Feel its shining and sunshine heart.
For even in the summer it rains
And my own sunset meets my own regret
And I wish some more for that red sky
To precede a golden mourning.
My sunlight cannot shine alone
I need my rainbow.

And looking up
I saw the sky transcend
Into a Noah's arc of children
For we are all children of light
And there will always be a rainbow for me
And that rainbow is my own nativity.

Paul Wright

A STATUE IN PORTUGAL

(To the sculptor - Vitor Picanco)

What a life
Here and there I go, all the day long do this, do that
My feet and hands are worn out
My head is full of worry and care, all the day long and all the night too

But I have joy
Walking to the broad waters of the river Alte
Looking back at my village, shining white in the sun
Standing in the cool water, as it sings to the stones
As the breeze plays music to the almond trees
Nature paints God's picture, sings His music, chants His verses
The hills shelter me round and protect

The strawberry trees are darkly evergreen, brooding
Thick glossy serrated leaves are handsome, my fine sons
Their white bell flowers, my graceful daughters
Red fruits make liquor, pure and strong, my husband
The riverside is a garden of earthly delights

I make a plea to Heaven
For a great eagle to put out the light of my life with its wings
And take me away, now my bitter toil is full
For my sorrow is profound and exquisite
I desire to be one with my beloved Algarve
To be one with the light, the air, the waters, the hills

My heart yearns to remain here, where I come each day to launder
To stay on this spot, through the day and through the night
To be as marble in everlasting ecstasy
The Algarve sun will rise upon me from the hills
For ever and ever

I have no head full of worry
No hands full of work, no feet full of journeys
I am just here, in the water with my heart -
Not as a worn out laundress
But a young woman with new small breasts
Untroubled by this demanding world

Be strong for your own struggle
Be holy and faithful; let God's fire consume you
Gaze at me and muse -
God is great, God is beautiful.

Derek Norris

SHARING A DRINK

Reflected in a glass of wine,
resplendent colours sparkle forth,
each one dancing off cut crystal facets
shimmering and prismatic;
Gold to show the priceless nature of our love,
crimson the depths
to which our thoughts run, like venous blood.
A shimmer of light green recalls the life
of natural world surrounding us,
beautiful, simple and yet complex.
The azure and sapphire could be love-given gems
exchanged and cherished, sky-blue and divine.
Patterns revolve, return and settle, like the glance
of each for each in other's eyes.
Where were you, all my early days, before
the vines were even planted, which produced
these glorious colours, tastes and senses?
You must have always been there somewhere,
for so great a pairing never could have been
fully divided, or merely chance.

J M Gardener

ANGELS DO WALK THIS EARTH

As you lay there in my arms
I didn't really see what I had in you,
I saw your beauty on the outside
But couldn't see what you had within,
You must have showed it many times
But at these times I was blinded,
Only now I see clearly, now that you're not with me
That your inner beauty was all
I ever needed to make my life complete.

Mark Mawson

LET US PRAY

Our father who art in fashion
Hallowed be thy style
Thy collection come
Thy show be done
On the catwalk
As it is on the street
Give us this day our attire
And forgive us our attitude
As we forgive those who have
Attitude against us
And lead us not into the capital
But deliver us from London
For thine is the collection
The cut and the shape
Formever and ever
Amen.

Philip McClenaghan

STEAM TRAINS

Gone are the days of the smut filled air
When a journey by rail meant a blackened face
The excitement that tingled the choking smoke
The thrill of delight as the whistle whooshed!
Like a star in the night that falls forever
My heart leaps, then falls, where it may.
Now clinical and pristine the soft grinding wheels
Begin their travel to the next shuddering stop.
But sometimes in their swaying passage
An innate memory struggles to the surface
And a shriek is heard like a banshee's wail
They are crying for the past of long ago
And they call for the trains of yesteryears
The loneliness becomes more than overwhelming
As desperately they seek the ghosts of the gone
The friends who had passed with an eerie scream.

Anne Szczepanska

THE UNACHIEVABLE DREAM

The day, drawn away from the night wove past
I felt its soul, overwhelming its misery,
so depressing as leeching its black hole
and the latest beam light
flowing out of my bleeding heart.

You abandoned me.

You dropped me without breath without the shower, without hope.

Why? I ask myself without an end
and I can't find the answer.
Without you I am as canvas without a mast
as a night sky without the stars.

I find that the gloom overwhelms me,
I suffer.
My dream remains unfulfilled,
I drown.
The tears report my face
I hear your voice on the radio
The solace doesn't come but my heat is torn.

I gaze at our photograph
the memories fly out in my mind.

Happy ever but never more
is it blame, that I feel
or my soul searching for explanation
overwhelmed by despair?
Fly in one better time when
together we laughed
as two connate others who had found themselves in the endless world.

The past,
everything has bobbed under in oblivion
and the now sluices me as a tidal wave.
The dream future, traversed by the fog, flies inaccessible,
it dissolves before my gaze.

Remain, I remain here and the words immerse me to the now,
the dream finds its chimney corner in my heart.

Well preserved from the gloom.
I regale in the cold rainy days, a glimmer of hope
a well from which, yes, you go unachievable.

The voice on the radio, the dream, the drive impracticable . . .

Ariadna Sinclair

MY THOUGHTS

My life, my reflection, my thoughts, my individuality.
People don't understand where I am coming from but I refuse to inflict my
situation on them, instead I choose to make my situation make me stronger.
I am maturing with life, I am battling with pain, I am crying with grief
but most importantly I am growing and overcoming hurdles which I face,
running along with this human race.
I am a queen; I stand as tall as a tree,
Higher than my imagination can take me.
You are my king as loving and as considerate as one can be,
I finally realise what has always been in front of me.
Just like a magnet we attract this statement I refuse to retract.
I have a voice as loud as a hyena, as powerful as a lion,
My roar will never cease to amaze, my inner strength one could not describe
Myself, my ideas what you see I am . . .
My pride.
I refuse to be made a statistic, I am an individual, I am a dream.
I know everything is not as simple as it may seem, but I am my individual dream.
Behind my shades, I hide my eyes that's because I don't want to view your lies.
I'm tired of crying, tired of upset and life's inconstant joys.
Men acting like little boys, girls thinking they are ladies and at twelve bearing
babies.
I tire of life's simple phases
But through my thoughts, my individuality, I know you will wake up and see the
reality.

Adria Lancaster

DELILAH

Moon-breasted, peach-skinned men
were captivated by her sensual thighs,
her open lips. He was
a toy before her tongue, her ploy to twist
his plan, the while they slept
in roses, foxes burning Gaza's corn.

He in his lion strength,
tender as honey in her bed, boasted
of how an ass' head
made donkeys of a thousand men; bowstrings
were soft as woollen threads.
Her foe, how should a woman bring him low?

New rushes on the floor,
sweet perfumed oils, her hair loose as a maid;
calf meat with cherries, silk
to lie in. Softly wove his seven braids
into her loom, cried, 'See
the Philistines!' and laughing he shook free.

It was the crescent moon
he broke his vow, licked grapes between her breasts;
so no more lies were told
and bold she shaved his sleeping head. His eyes
they stole, bound him in iron.
Blinded, as Gaza's slave he ground their corn.

As burning oil her pain
to learn of Dagon's feast, him mocked, chained like
a beast, his chest whipped sore.
Yet proud that he stood tall, cried to his God
between the pillar heads,
and lonely was her grief when Samson died.

Kathy Butler

THE MEMORY BAG

A fleeting tug of a rein as I play gee-up.
The pleasurable pain of picking a scab.
A queenly pose in a fist padded bra,
The sickening lurch when first love falls.

The memory bag starts to fill.
The rose-petal feel of a newborn ear.
Chaotic mornings, breakfast go!
Crying times, laughing times, pride
In watching our chicks grow.

No time to think of the memory bag.

Divorce, - all passions twisted,
Shredded love, life fragmented.
Past anchors lost as parents die.
Heavy life is crawling by.

Won't think of the memory bag.

Time turns, travel beckons.
Smooth thick Russian vodka,
Turquoise icebergs, chinstrap penguins,
Vibrant India, piquant spices.

Memory bag bulging now.

The memory bag is almost ovoid.
Corrugated brain-shaped mass.
Fizzing, sparkling, speeding colours
Changing, buzzing, whizzing round.

At least I think it is,
I don't use it much these days.
I'm not sure where it is,
I'm not sure if it is.

It's fading
Slipping, sliding astray,
Going away,
Turing gr . . .

Sheila Wicks

WISE CONFUSION

Sometimes we speak without thinking,
Sometimes we think without speech.
Learning the language of reason
So often remains out of reach.

Searching each face for a clue there,
Struggling for clarity's gift.
Seeking an all-knowing answer
But always that deep chasmic rift.

Tranquil the mental oblivion,
Inwardly smiling with ease.
Patronising in tolerant fashion,
Fragment memories repeatedly tease.

Reciting unanswerable questions,
Impossible veils to conceal.
Play the system, don't invite rejection -
What they probe for we'll never reveal.

Patti Robertson

LAST SNOWS

Diamond glitter, winter lingers,
Ocean dancing
Water white.
Secret beauty, frantic fever,
Petals flutter
Catch the light.
Fleeting footfalls, foxes shiver,
Crystal swans
Arise in flight.
Ghostly breathing, darkness thickens,
Firelight shadows
Shade the night.

Stephanie Harris

DANCED WITH THE DEVIL

She danced the last flamenco with me
We turned in that Spanish town square
The stars shone bright
As did the flowers in her hair

I was dizzy and confused
But all I focused on was She
So I did not notice the palpable mist
Of evil in the air

That band played out
As if their souls possessed
When the lights flickered I felt a shiver
Her beauty was surely rare

Something was wrong though I remember
The other revellers looked scared
As I danced so oblivious
Foreign whispers pierced the air

Finally the dance it ended
She slipped away I knew not where
And the passion that I felt
Seemed to end right there

On waking the next day
Order had been restored
Yes it all seemed so magical
That night we could have been a pair

Right then I vowed to find her
I was bewitched you see
She took my heart then discarded
And didn't seem to care

Time's gone by and I've lost hope
I'll not find her now I'm sure
She vanished like a spectre
This parting I must bear

Now a piece of my soul is lost
I blame it all on She
I must have danced with the Devil
In that quaint old Spanish square.

Paul Llewellyn

MY FOREVER AUTUMN

Autumn leaves of gold and brown
Litter the Earth's floor
I dream of my angel
Beaming with beauty

The eyes of my angel shine
Your bright smile brings warmth
To my heart and very soul
Such a beautiful spirit

There are those who
Bring out the best in us
You are one of those
To help someone find their heart
And open their mind's eye is a gift

Winter wind bites my face
A tear almost frozen in time
My angel is decorated in scarf and hat
The wind a little colder than before

Emotion so powerful it removes breath
I stop to collect air
You breathe and smile
Your beauty preserved forever

As we stumble through leaves and snow
We battle our worries and fears
We strive to be all we dream
We gaze at the clock watching and waiting

You are so beautiful
Your heart strong and loving
A faith unmoveable
You smile; your hand brushes your hair
Our beautiful love
Stands tall a shining beacon forever.

Jonathan Curry

A LONG WAY FROM HOME

A slow moving river reflects
An image of a place I knew
The distant fisher casts a line
With no hope of a catch

My thoughts mull around
So many wasted opportunities
I am another distant fisher
Who would net a reflection

Yet these clumsy hands create
Mere ripples on the mirror
Causing one more child to cry
A long way from home

I sleep tho' dreams give no rest
The guilt awaits another morning
Scant hiding place under this star
Is this our long threatened Hell?

Paradise without a moment's peace
A reflection appearing to mock
Everlasting reminders of our lives
Lived with undue care for self

No holy day here to repent
Just eternity left to ponder
On the wrong road leading to
A long way from home.

John Marshall

CO-HABITATION

Late April, early May,
Sprays and sweet scents of lilacs
And no less of bluebells
Giving their all
To herald the advent of spring,
And early roses
Soon blue tits and much maligned favour hued
Starlings and coal tits arrive
Each looking for sustenance
For young and siblings, in the rafters and around
My house, my loft and thus my garden blessed,
So I live with these my friends and acquiesce
To share
But wary of each other's presence
Each giving only brief cognition of our present state,
Some leave midsummer for another mate,
And thus to various alienate
So we live in nature's harmony
Around and in
Our home
In much tranquillity.

Dai C Davies

SOMETHING FAINT AND FAR AWAY

Something faint and far away
something I loved.

'Did you - do you exist in reality?'
I ask the fleeting dream or long past memory.
'I did - I do.'
A recent dream is so like something in the past - the long past.

The struggle to remember is the same,
Sometimes, something stands out but this one is so faint and far away and yet so
poignant.
Is it from my childhood home or longer past or Heaven?

Something faint and far away something I loved.

Jacqueline Ives

SANCTUARY

Sleekly insinuating in the cloistered quiet
of stone sarcophagi and pillared peace.
Slit-eyed in the gloom, with noiseless purpose
he investigates unnoticed crevices, and peers
unhurriedly beneath each cloth and canopy.
Transcending church delineations and protocol,
sombrely, sensuous, soft tail caresses
pews and pulpit base with indiscriminate
delight. Each a known, familiar landmark
in his daily pilgrimage of recognition -
with haughty disregard of cantilevered excellence.
Ignoring choral chants, cantatas, all the notes
of harmony from cherub-ruffled boys.
Fed, not on transubstantiated bread and wine,
but on piscatorial fantasies and verger's milk
left daily, secretly, beside the transept door.
Pontificating priests, breath-rimed in frosty air,
or canting cleric's lulling summer voice
receive no muted mystical response
from ears attuned to rodent rustlings.
This unfazed feline form slinks heedlessly
among the Bishop's copes and cassock cloths.
Back arched in ecstasy of sensuous display
as vestry garbs provide the musty means
of momentary, kittenish regressive play.
His dignity restored, face washed, resuming
exploration of his sovereign territory,
he surveys the chancel; dappled altar front
kaleidoscoped in stained glass prismed light.
A paw bats idly at a dancing shaft of blue,
but transitory entertainment holds no thrall.
The insubstantial shadows of the darkened depths
invite his furtive green-eyed fascination.
Intricate and sculpted choir stalls, with patina of age
looks suitably recessed and with a leap
the black and white furred form attains his goal,
turns in concentric circles, yawns and sinks in apathy,
to sleep in virtuous peace.
Surveillance now completed, duty done
and haven thus achieved with equanimity,
Cathedral cat reposes.

Anne M Smithers

LEFT BEHIND

The first, the last
Lay sleeping, lay silent
Looking up, looking above.
Telling a tale
A tale of a man
Who will not dance
Or tremble with fear
But who will
Sit alongside
Roaring with laugher.
Wild and free
Black tight curls lay
Upon his head.
Disappearing again and again
A smile forever and always.
Like seasons gone by
With each new day
Lives cling together
Into the sea of fate
And gaze, moving, dancing,
Glittering like diamonds.
The lion's heart taken
But so glorious in the sun.
Remember - no regrets
Unconscious spirit
Forever a life
The complete man.

Sharron Hollingsworth

POETRY SAYS

Odes are musical with a certain rhyme
Epics tell stories and tales of any time
Sonnets often speak of love and life
saying fourteen lines only you most write
making sure when counting
you get it right.
Lyrics to sing in metre and mood
don't try the tune if the voice isn't good.
Limericks too have a place on the page
Just one stanza in humour
to keep the pace.
Monologue, this is your big chance
if you feel confident today
for only one speaker is needed to say.
Blank verse, write down how you feel
every thought, every whim
remember, ten syllables to stretch each line
this is the catch if you only have nine.
An elegy very often is sad to relate
sometimes treasures an important date.
Soliloquy will cheer you up
for this means you can talk to yourself.
Forget about all this terminology today
just write down the words in ribbons and strands
weaving and sewing into a coloured stanza.

Hazel Wilson

AT TWENTY

Life
Calls out
With alokos[1] guttural gong:
Spreads mats, spreads palm,
Spreads thorns for my diffident feet.

Iku[2] lurks
In the waiting sea, with eyes
Of fiendish passion
With arms of restless probing.

Iku lurks . . .
And every tick-tock
Of yeasty years, of eastering suns,
Every tick-tock of roaming moons
Snowballs in the vaults of my brain.

Life
Is calling . . .
A loyal beard clings firmly
To the bosom of my chin,
Firmly

And cupid ogles
With the fangs of her sickle.

My nose shelters the rim
Of thick-framed lenses;
I peep through these,
I peep through
And see the world no longer round.

> No longer round
> The world shrinks now
> Into a brutesome crescent,
> The world shrinks

And saviours beckon:

> Some speak of bliss
> On the breath of powdery grains,
> Of eternal bliss on re-birth
> Like sucking neonates.

> Some hold out fronds of arcane syntax,
> Some speak of gods, some arrogant as gods

And they speak
Oh how they speak!

Life is calling . . .
And several roads and several lanes
And several paths spread before my feet
Like the roundabout of Ojuelegba[3].

Which is lamp, which is light . . . ?

[1] A bird with a high-pitched voice
[2] The Yoruba word for Death
[3] A winding crossroads in Lagos.

Michael Afolabi Sylfad

UNBROKEN CIRCLE

Explosion of birth, maturation of life
Natural progression
Unstoppable cycle
Nursery school and college strife
Meeting of partners, forging ahead
Explosion of birth, maturation of life
Forging ahead with new paths to pursue
Siblings competing for attention and lead.
Interacting, exchanging their views to survive
Natural progression
Unstoppable cycle
Explosion of birth, maturation of life
Time roller coasting
As season follows season
Buds bursting forth from winter's cloak
New life
Generation after generation
In fragility and strength.
Explosion of birth, maturation of life
Unbroken circle.

Gael Nash

A MIDSUMMER DREAM

Last night I dreamed a dream, wherein
I drifted to a sunlit spot
Where flower fragrance filled the air
Awakening senses long forgot

The sound of laughter echoed there
Companions, innocents at play
The place was magical and yet
Oblivious to all were they

Under the trees I sought the shade
The lush green turf became my bed
Where blackbirds stirred beneath the hedge
And bees buzzed softly overhead

A brook sang somewhere near at hand
I recognised its melody
And I became one with the land
Where Earth and sky seemed part of me

Then I awakened with a start
To my chagrin I care to say
Though filled with longing to return
Alas I could not find the way

But on reflection I have learned
The long well-known and simple truth
That time and place are transient
The time was past, the place was youth.

E Urmston

JACK HAMMER

A Jack hammer
has a steel-tipped nose, handle-grips for ears
and a long rubber hose so it can breathe
and it's heavy.

It spits and blasts cold, wet air
you pull on its trigger
and compressed air comes shooting through its nostrils.

You haul a Jack
and drag it around
point it at stone and it'll take you down
into concrete
and it'll shake you.

A Jack hammer
echoes everywhere
raking your bones
and deafening the air
with a heavy metal rifling
sort of a noise
like a machine gun
and you need ear plugs.

As well as strength in your
arms to steady it upright
and a grasp of both handles
to angle the bit
for chipping, cracking and breaking
up floors or to pull it out.

But in terms of tools
there's no better way
to make the ground crumble
beneath your feet.

Kevin Meehan

MRS BRUCE'S CASTLE

I love Wilton Grange.

Enter and behold the surprise,
Open your eyes.
Just look at it,
Just stare,
A house like this
In West Hartlepool
Less than a mile from town?
So unexpected,
So inexplicable,
Eclecticism gone mad
But oh so beautiful,
So fitting.
Arts and crafts of centuries
Mixed in the same cauldron
Rest in state in an Edwardian refuge,
Safe and comforting - built to last.
A churchy feeling of awesome magnificence
Yet homely - full of the past
Yet! A battleground where campaigns
Private and public have been fought
And won.

A place full of secrets
Encompassed in time's fist.
A sort of place of history - of fun and tragedy,
A place of people from otherwhere.

Wave a magic wand
See it all appear
An inglenook bell
Rings in a servant's ear.
An elegant lady transcends
Wide shallow stairs.
No need to lift her trailing skirt
As she treads unawares.
Magic!
Then they are gone . . .

A magic house.

Sheila Bruce

REPLY

Goddess
Thank you for your letter.
I thought it would never come.
But when I woke this morning
that line of migrant geese
written in fluid ink by your idiosyncratic hand
on the clean page of a new day
made me feel young again.

Whose script but yours
could so skilfully depict
the buds unzipping on each bough?
The page exudes your presence.
Now winter's dirty newsprint
melts into the stream's calligraphy
flowing between banks arabesqued with celandine.

When last I walked those banks
dog's mercury had risen,
but no coltsfoot lit dead leaves.
Today I thrill, anticipating
with you days to come;
inebriant bees in poppy heads,
the swift's rapt return;
but that is distant yet.

Come, even as Man's apish hand
all innocence lost, deflowers Earth.
The ice caps melt, seas rise.
The angry gods urge Pluto
to lock you forever in Hell's grot.
Lady, rejuvenate our innocence
as guidance for this cunning hand
to bring Earth new fruitfulness.

Come, as all life from slumber wakes,
and bid Man burst his wintry tomb.
I wake and wait. Write again tomorrow,
but tell no one we are lovers.
I kiss your signature, Persephone.
Tonight, I will fold your page
Beneath my pillow - hoping
for Arcadian dreams. Farewell.

Terence Smith

ONE ROAD TO FREEDOM

Do you know what it feels like to be oppressed?
To be chained to a fate that lies not in your palms, but within the palms
                                        of your greatest enemy?
Your life and dreams stamped upon until they become like scattering dust.
Your overwhelming desire to taste freedom unquenched until your dying day.
Tell me oh Mankind, do you truly know what freedom is worth?
Freedom is the balance to all things.
It is the shield worn by great warriors,
And the dream envisaged by noble leaders.
Freedom is the flag of one nation standing side by side in vision,
It is the timeless carving upon the walls of history,
Which are looked upon favourably by the eyes of tomorrow,
And protected by the gentle palms of today.
Freedom is the story spoken by struggle,
And the medal worn by unseen heroes.
Freedom, is the purpose of existence that enriches meaningless lives with cause,
Blessing the Earth with justice, truth and reminding the hearts of godly sight,
Freedom is the wind that carries the seed of hope and gently laces it
                                        into the arid land,
Absorbing it from all darkness and enlightening the skies with brilliance.
Freedom is the anchor that routes all men to one point,
Uniting hearts and inspiring minds,
Evoking tears and embracing lives.
Freedom is one language spoken across a thousand shores,
It is the battered ship that sails relentlessly on through powerful storms.
Freedom is the mirroring balance that causes faces to smile,
Rather than to be drowned in unwanted frowns.
It is the golden crown worn by every man, woman and child,
And the timeless jewel buried beneath secret grounds.
Freedom is meaning and meaning is what the Earth rests upon,
Just like water that spreads through the land, wavering, tilting and
                                        shimmering,
Freedom is the route to all life,
It is the sustenance of every breath and the clasp of every hand,
The cure of every scar and the dream of every man.
It is the first words spoken and the last words uttered amongst battlefields,
Freedom is humanity at its greatest hour.
It is the coolness of the breeze against raging fires,
It is the gentleness of a mother's touch upon her child,
And the sincerity of a father's love against deadly desire.
Freedom is the open valley that opposes barbed wire,

And the brave roar in humiliating silence.
Oh how we are all born free,
But as our skin begins to age and our hearts begin to turn frail,
We mortals become chained to the commands of oppressors,
And soon we neglect the godly dream that once inspired us,
Yes, oh how we are all born free,
But the question remains, are we to die free or in unseen chains?

Seja Majeed

OFF THE BEATEN TRACK

(After a reproduction print of Loute-Algarve)

The hidden courtyard sleeps in the afternoon
sun under a halcyon sky;
nothing moves in siesta hour except three cats;
the Good the Bad and the Ugly; one sits
watching as the others skulk from the shadows
over warm cobblestones like gunslingers;
tension builds to a crescendo before the showdown.

A resident wakes from a drowse to look
at the scene from her window; thoughts lost
in her bucolic dream under olive trees.
Later, she prepares fish, onions, garlic,
peppers and tomatoes for a stew; stirs in
goodwill and spices, sets the table,
placing a dish of olives on a white doily.

A smile crosses her face when she feeds
the cats; she thinks of the evening,
the blessing of family and friends.

Lynn Brookes

THIS ROPE

We are this double twined
and boy scout knotted rope
which runs from my belly button,
via my boy scout knotted heart,
to you.

Both our hands are thickly callused
and chunky with the scars
of salt seared sores from
clinging grimly onto it,
in storms.

I have battled
with it wrapped around my knuckles,
while clouds groaned like full bellies overhead.
The weight of our years in water
soaking through my childhood parka,
and my teenage tracksuit tops
to you.

It soaks through the present
of my wool-blend vintage cardi
to my skin,
which is knitted and purled
from the molecules and follicles
of you.

So we are damply tangled
with byzantine intricacy
by the last of our past
and this rope.

So that when we struggle,
or just heavily sigh,
it tightens and snags and digs and chafes,
into memories and breast bones
and elbows and thighs.

We are too big now
for this labyrinth of debt,
this mess of flesh,
and my heavy guilt sorry chest
and you.

We are this fractious, boisterous awkward love,
whose embers have glowed grimly
in the rain-sloppy mud.
But who knows whether
we can weather
sunny days?

This rope is welting my wrists
but this hope is melting my heart.
Softly, softly my willpower lingers,
but with chilly damp fingers
I am gently untangling
this rope.

Sally Jenkinson

THREE BOYS

(Sixty years on)

We spoke on the phone a month before
You died;
We agreed to meet in Tunbridge Wells,
We lied.

You wanted to talk on soldier poets
In line
But I heard the bugle call 'Last Post'
This time.

On our meeting day you could not go,
Regret.
Tunbridge Wells and I knew you did not
Forget.

Schoolboy days and evacuation,
Mixed joys.
Amongst the mourners following you -
Three boys.

Alan Dickson

LAST

The sun bleached skeleton of our love
lies obsolete between us,
its fingers entwined with ours
turning to chalk as we try
to breathe a last breath into it.

I didn't know we'd fallen
until the concrete broke my bones,
firing pain into my eyes
and stopping my heart
from beating a last beat
inside

before it's thrown up in front of me
and lies like a bloodied corpse.
What else is there for me
dying here,
no last beat, no last breath
at all.

Kay Middleditch

GRAINS

Listen to the unwritten grains,
This moment is worth many grains.
Love escapes like a memory
                Lured away by time,
                Only to return
As an echo of something less.

All grains of unwritten future,
Is light showing the way ahead.
A faint voice hidden in the breeze:
                Listen to the grains
                Killing the nightmare
Of a cold predestined future.

Krister Andersson

KEEP QUIET

'Keep quiet.'
What binds us but the fiery terror?
What keeps our souls entwined?
Love is strong
but times are tough
we won't be 'we' for long.

'Keep quiet.'
We're a violent trance
away from the chance
to break the tattered thread.

A breath away
from the golden hour
when we are 'we' no more.

'Keep quiet.'
There's nothing like misery to open the doors
that once kept darkness at bay.
What are we, now?
What are we?
Now that we're not 'we'.

Aseel Mohamed Ahmed Bala

VANITY

Caustic words nonchalantly spoken
Your indifference leaves me broken
Reflection points to your conceit
. . . Selfish, greedy . . . yet forgiven?
A mockery of me, my heart and all
Pensively fought . . . Oh how I fall
Irony ponders this mockery of me
Self-defamation my one vanity!

Shah Wharton

BARONESS

His name was Bond,
James Bond.

Posing at the bar stand
the dashing suave bachelor,
with sparklers for teeth.
Dazzling
on his beautiful, chiselled face.

We met at the oil baron's gala.
My devious rhinestone dress
teased his attention across the parlour.
Goldeneyes.
I pulled out my compact,
prepared my war paint
and marched to his spot at the bar.

I had every notion
of seeking cheap pleasure that night,
and after too many unpaid vodkas,
Bond became a target
within my sight.

Next thing I recall,
we were crashing and stumbling
at his penthouse door.
The booze settled,
and we were eager for more.

Desperate for that famous touch,
my brazen scarlet lips dived in.
I recall, that to my pleasure
he returned the favour.
But his clown-like hands
fumbled for my zip,
his lips ready to savour.

Then a shot to my eyes!
with that gadget he triggered.
I stifled all cries.
He was limp, lame and lacklustre.
He tried and yet,
sex with him had me wonder.
Why was his fabled sword
famed for being longer?

I felt shaken
but not stirred.
I yearned for raw passion,
His stained breath
on his hyper tongue,
lingered upon a cocktail of martinis
and Cuban cigars.
Which I knew
were a farce.

Morning came.
Thankfully.
I had never been so grateful
of just amber glow
Beyond the pearly panes.
I turned to James Bond,
my shame.

His slender frame was sprawled
across the silks
snoring gently.
Clearly pleased with the previous night,
when the sword appalled.

Then his eyelids rose,
glistened
and dare I say it he farted.
That's right, farted!
That was the final straw,
time that I departed.

Farewell James
you're not the man I need.
I want a villain,
ravenous for the feed.
I hear Jaws is looking . . .

Azize Bozkurt

WORDS, WORDS, WORDS

(Hamlet, Act 2. Scene 2. Line 191)

The detritus
Of our imagination,
Precipitating out
In harsh
And catalytic fluids
Of reality.
Swirls
In the aimless
Currents of uncertainty
Into a patchwork
Of perfidy and perfection.

We pick
With ever conscious care
From each word-laden shelf
In nightmare's
Stockroom:
But what we choose
Could just as easily be read
From whirling numeric balls
And bingo calls.

The colours of the rainbow
Flash against those balls
Where long ago
They flickered in the spray.

Full circle
Is the trite and facile phrase
That many now would say
But we!
We are light-years removed
Even from yesterday!

Jeffrey Amor Pickford

HOLIDAY MEMORIES OF MALTA

Dawn is breaking, nothing disturbs the surface
of the calm, blue Mediterranean sea.
The pale blue of the sky, mingling with
the azure clear water of the sea, is a sight too beautiful to behold.
The sun, just peeping out from beyond the horizon,
throws a shimmering glow on the vast area of the bay below me.

It's late afternoon now
The blue colours of the sky and sea, mingle wonderfully
with the local yellow stone of which the buildings are made of.
The intensity of the hot sun, sends a beautiful glow
on the rocky plateaux that form the islands of Malta, Gozo and Comino.

The rugged outline, hides a wonderful blend of villas, hotels and farms.
There is beauty all around me, beauty, if one cares to look beyond the rough
surface of the islands.
History is evident, everywhere one looks,
History which dates back thousands of years, mingle
With modern technology, hiding the most wonderful tapestry
Of old buildings, old towns and villages.

Mary-Magdalene Kiddie

BEFORE I DEPART

Before I depart I will show you all of me.
Not the mere outer layer but the light that brings life and enlightenment.
I'm not alone but yet no one is there to share my words or to care
for me in despair.
Maybe you were never there or maybe I should not care or dare
stare at the man I have become.
Humanity will show me the stone path of true knowledge not your
words or books.
Your look and faces I see though like it traces, paper with two sides
Can easily be erased in stages.

Shane Jordan

PREDATOR

With hidden claws he prowled the winter dark
Hunting with consummate ease.
Lithe, alert, with pool-deep eyes,
He caught small prey
And brought it home,
A trophy to his skill.

What did he know of its small life
Of quiet peace in dappled sun,
The raising of a tiny brood
Among the leaves?
What did he care?

It moved,
He pounced,
It moved no more
And he prowled on
To bigger things.

Fran Barker

RED

Did the flames mock you
while you stoked a hunger for
the red you stole from where?
From everywhere. Cloth,
plastic, minds, paper.
Did the sparks spit their scorn
for your eyes as they hinted
carmine, crimson, scarlet?
Embers glowing a heated
reminder of who you had become.
Had the fire, conspired its heat,
its smoke, it's anger, turned your
already molten logic in on you,
burnt you, scorching the smoulder
of what remained of you, turning
again your heat, blood, eyes -
Red?

Mark Thirlwell

UNTITLED

I've thought about it; love
What an eternal affair!
Less like the dirty feeling
Of the droning fading stamp from drunk's door.
The printed regret of yesterday
The stubborn stain of tomorrow
Less like this
But somewhat still a part of love.

And because I've thought about it, love
I mean,
I've crept into the sweetness of some poor man's dance
We've played hide-and-seek
Behind towers of fabric, intertwined with battered air
And half breath laughter
Remembering that you have had a dream
It was of love
But it was not like this

Oh yes, I've thought about love
The scar, the scratch on the vinyl of existence
We die to find it
Failed in the quest
A search for love's destruction
A search to cry broken tears
On my mother's shoulder

Thinking about love, yes
It has skinned me and grated me
Forced me to crush the la de das
Yet my terror wanes and leaves perhaps distorted room
For me to ask you
Where have you been?
I've grown a soul so damp!
Are those grey hairs around Cupid's arrow?
You seem to have a different motive
Perhaps it's right for me now, for me mature
What clarity!
I sigh.
Oh love, I've missed you.

Keri Holt

COLOURS OF A KISS

A kiss is . . .
A cornucopia of ripe, fresh fruit
Juicy, sweet and soft of touch
Never too much
To peel the skin
To its yummy, pulpy, dribbling core
Jolt sensual and sublime within

A kiss is . . .
The stabbing of a thousand knives
That pierce the skin and plunge the heart
To sorrowful, painful, lonely parts
Irretrievable, untouched, here and now
Thinking, spasming
Eventually numb

A kiss is . . .
A whisper kept and stored forever
Haunting daydreams, enshrouding nights
Entombed in memories, savoured hours
That belonged to us
Was great, was ours
If you'd only whisper one more time
All I asked that once was mine

A kiss is . . .
A darkened cave of promises
That lit its lamps with every step
Ignited, woke what's honest, prized
A glistening hoard of treasure troves
Enduring, potent, galvanized

A kiss is . . .
A rotting corpse of cold regret
Stenched and bloodied
Skin all peeling with rancid reek
An oral autopsy, death's decay
To think these lips can kiss, can speak

A kiss is . . .
The song we thought would never end
Not tire, tuneless, trite
But bar by bar and note by note
Sings swift and sultry

Always fresh with each recital
We practised often, knew by rote

A kiss is . . .
The man I knew I always was
Unveiled by such a simple act
My mask slid off, the flesh was free
Unequivocally the real me, dignified
Enriched, enhanced and not ashamed
All I wished - personified

A kiss is . . .
A blinding, itching cataract
Stinging, jabbing, blurring vision
Cackling scorn and cruel derision
Thinking sight is what you have (deceived!)
Eyes with which you want to see
Sliced open wide by love's incision

A kiss is . . .
The pulse which giddies heart and mind
Bravely unbounded by its bliss
Can there ever be enough of this
Sweet and sour
Hot and cold
Good and bad
Light and dark
Many-sided, multi-mooded
Valiant, vicious
Elegant, coarse
Grand, ignoble
Heroic, ignominious

Once and infinitesimal - to taste such
Lip-locked loveliness
Turning back the clock no more
Full-throttled, fiery, awe and shock
Synapses kicking, punching, screaming
A kiss released, a kiss unlocked.

Jamie Caddick

ESCAPADE

11:16 along a rooftop,
Creeping backlit by harvest moon
Hanging high over darkened fields
And the ghosts of sheep,

Drunk on slippery orange beam
And guided by Polaris' watchful eye,
I point-dance upon apex
And weathervane's arrow.

Illicit through glass and charged
Top-full with mandragora,
I usher you into sweet sleep
Make metronome your breathing.

And, slipping back into the
Embrace of that epic orb,
I retrace glistening, fervent steps
And curl back into skin
To wait.

Kathleen O'Farrell

MAIKO

Serpents stretched in mercury creeping
Midnight wraps a formless art
Bronze white folds tied at the back declaring chastity
Fleeting nods of bobbing meaning.

Soulful orbs hidden then revealed by sweeping movement
Every elegant paced step a story revealed.
Shimmering black crowns a ghostly pale visage born for candles
Apple lips parted in lonely whispered service

Han'gyoku Maiko dancing teasing tradition
Seducing rejection of tradition's wanton advance
Kyoto demure measured daughter Maiko
Tradition's favoured child.

Alexis Dalton

SHE WHO HATH ROSES WITHIN HER CHEEKS

Wilt thou join then hand in mine,
Choose me for thy fireside companion?
For I long to see the roses within thine cheeks
That glow only in response to heat?
Indeed, it pleaseth me to observe one so fair;
Flame-kissed when flames mock love's true glow.
I wonder, wouldst thou dare to sit so bold
If thou couldst know of all who gaze?

So whereupon our eyes feast hence,
I entreat thee not to move an inch.
Unless thine eyes be blackened coals
And unlike my heart you speakest in jest?
Hadst I not a pilgrim's soul,
I would take the ashes whereon the hearth they lay,
And cast them amongst those in my grate
In hope that, in ash, thine shadow's robbed;
And if thus, let it forever be
That my own shadow ne'er stray from thee!

Samantha Crossley

A NEWER - AN DER FERNCE GELIEBE

Fair countryside of peace and beauty lies
Where all the trees shake leaves in understanding
And wink pale petals at my heart's complaining.
Thus doth I fill my soul with heartfelt sighs
And know that lonely and alone I'll rise
To greet anew, another pointless dawning.
No! I shall, my planned intents now scorning,
Return to feast my eager, aching eyes
Upon my single, priceless prize
And plead my hopeless love, yet kneeling,
Ask my 'Belle Dame sans Merci' for my healing
With words that on a lover's lips arise.
Cupid fix your sharp arrow to your string
Pierce my flesh that again my heart may sing.

Derrick John Silver

THE LANE

A sinuous stretch of charcoal. Tufts of grass, pock-marking tarmac
that crumbles into damp earth and verdant green.
Framed by trees and grass - growing things
over-arched by shifting moods of blue and grey and black.

Breathe -
A rank, pungently pervasive wild garlic reek.
Aching newness, buds of fragile yellow, brittle blue.
Unsteady, untried knock-kneed bleating, doused with
blobs of rain, cold, hope drenched bleak.

Breathe -
Acrid summer storms, a scorched Earth trail.
Eternal blue buffed by puffs of wisp.
Bubbling, babbling swallows streamed in flight.
Warm wind like a clammy, careless exhale.

Breathe -
A plumy bouquet of damp, mouldering leaves.
Motion frozen into doe eyes, twitching ears
that flick the small sounds of dwindling life.
Cold, sharp as a slap, fringing twigs into relief.

Breathe -
Fired oil blends tendrils of wood smoke
that finger a frail, palsied leaf.
The vocal anger of swollen water
suppressed by cold into stillness.
Hold, hold, and wait with dormant hope . . .

Helen Stockton

MISCOMMUNICATION

Talking to you
Is like mouthing through plate glass,
Or wearing someone else's spectacles:
A preposition's tiny sparkle,
Swells up huge as castle towers,
A once brave booming diphthong shrinks ashamed.

I wonder if
I've not left in last night's plugs,
And shake this morning's shower from my ears,
But still you seem to speak in code, a
Cryptic cacophony of ill-orchestrated sound
That jars like clumsy cubes in perfect holes.

Or it could be
That we're being sabotaged,
Our communications cruelly scrambled
By a swarm of microscopic gnats,
Whose tiny wings like grains of sand
Let only airy hollow vowels sneak through.

But I suspect
We speak in riddles, circling
Like wary beast a point we'd rather dodge.
Weak, we skirt a host of guessed-at hurdles
Brushing blame and grazing doubt,
Leaving blanks where simple honest words should be.

Jane Downs

FOR OUR FIRST DATE

For our first date
I suggested a walk in the woods . . .
but she branched out
when I wanted only
to put down roots.
So I took her to a local street market . . .
but she simply stalled.
Having faith . . .
I escorted her to Sunday worship
but as it turned out . . . I hadn't a prayer.
At the gourmet restaurant
we were slow to start . . .
lost our way during the main course
and then she desserted me.
Finally . . .
at the theatre
I discovered that it was all an act.
A mellow drama.
A meek tragedy.
A Freudian farce.
Love is so hard to define.

Trevor Crocker

HOMELESS CHILD

I remember a cosy house
Living with no fear.
But nowadays I'm scared,
In my eyes a droplet of tear

Always cold, begging for food
Every day I wake up with a foul mood
My life is a lonely road
With no spark of light . . .

Saloni Pun

COMING TO BLOWS

Spreading tendrils, creeping slowly
Resenting invasion of the nasty kind
Ever weeping, ne'er forgiving
Eating deep, within the mind

Weakening muscles, losing senses
Armour raised, but nothing reaches
Down weapons, frightening consequences
Mistaken life choice one teaches?

Restless night hours, just hall clock
Chiming - sensing shortly the end so close
Hopeless sculptures, impotent texts
Isolated, now think what matters most?

Stalking, falling, one faith's tainted
Anger at shields deflated, so many lows
Harassing slowly, ever wilder
This weary frame, soon no more prose.

Jan McGeachie

BLACKBIRD

Would I the power to unlock the beak
Pull from that black throat meaning to his song
Feather shod words muffled in language gone
Could I break nature's code and still complete
Riddle down echoes of magic now wrong

Where are you stranger? Be friendly and greet
For this morning to us only belongs
High in green eaves where the mystery's strong
To one bound to the ground feeling so weak
Send notes floating free afore ye fly on

The raven will speak to madmen and kings
With words flowing clear from the start
But blackbird talks through tunes that he sings
Heard not by the ear but the heart.

Ian Dixon

IN THE BELLY OF THE BEAST

Little tranquil white town
Salted on blue seas,
Its story is a woeful one
Of pain and miseries.
While children did cry sleeping,
And mothers cried awake,
Husbands did go creeping
The town's whores they did take.
The blacksmiths did much hammering but nothing did they make,
The bakers did much eating but nothing did they bake.
But sins can't dance forever,
Under covers they're so bare.
Wickedness can't endeavour,
Without catching the beast's dead stare.
So the beast did visit the town one night,
And stalked the town's scum under reddened lights.
'Sir, would you like to sample my delights?'
'Hello, for five coins only I could excite!'
The beast was so mortified he simply said,
'No, but thank you kindly,' and painted white town red.

Opening your eyes,
Wondering what went wrong,
So bitter and so despised,
Your heart beats out a new black song.
You were only happy when it rained,
Now the world passes on your parade,
You realise as you writhe in pain,
It's time that you sung out a new refrain.
Cos the rain's started falling and your flesh starts to burn,
An acrid smell on your nostrils which grates on the tongue,
You know the grass is much greener,
Wish your fat was much leaner.
As the pack comes to feed,
As your lips start to bleed,
With lies and screams,
And hate-filled dreams.

But they tear at your flesh and pluck it like hair,
And before you can scream your bones are sucked bare.
They laugh when you cry,
And they rot all your dreams.
'Stop! Stop!' you cry so madly,
'But we can't do that - you've behaved so badly!'
After some time your convulsions cease,
And the pack's hunger seems to ease,
'You've been so gracious as the host of our feast
We welcome more of your kind to the belly of the Beast.'

The victims you chose were alone,
Your hate bled into your bones,
Whether people were brown, black, fat or thin,
Whether they were ugly or just dark-skinned,
Slash-like eyes,
Flattened nose,
Fat-dripping thighs,
Or lacked your ego -
Which was, ironically, pretty fat,
It's hilarious thinking of the people you hated at,
Your heart is thin, its skin is black.
You were stinky with kind words,
Found it funny when they ripped,
When it came to spite,
Like a charity you'd give
But now you've sunk to the pit,
All the squalor and shit,
And you flap and you flit,
And you retch and you spit,
But the wings you so adored,
They can flap no more,
In their coffin of sludge,
Of tar-thick blood.
And the stench of stagnant flesh on the harlot's breath,
And the bitter curdled milk for her heaving breast,
All paraded back and forth like meat on a rack,
Till they fall amidst the other's upon great bloated stack,
Drowning in bodies oiled in hangman's sweat,
Which in turn dries on the noose which in turn hugs to the neck.
Your eyes fat and bloated of this offalous feast
You're so frail yet so despised in the belly of the beast.

Linden Feng

SPIN!

Spin!
Let blood skim
The skin you're in
Call pulse to flush
That lovely sash
Of flesh.

Run!
Soles and souls
With Earth imprint
Free the path -
Spring up and
Sprint!

Play!
A smile is miles
Of fresh horizon.
Be young,
Show your tongue
To troubles.

Spend!
Time is money
The best invest
In friends.
Make do and mend.
Listen, just be there -
You're a millionaire!

Love!
Pence can't save
The pound of heart
So start the melt:
Less critique
More turn of cheek
Less fits of pique
More easy speak . . .
Love, love, love!

Sing!
We sparrows gild
The morning ear -
'I'm here!'
Be heard
Little bird!

Dance!
Life's a gambol -
Take the chance,
A leap of faith.
Shake the hip and . . .
Skip!

And live!
Breathe . . .
Yours is the air
And glories everywhere.
Be glad and know
That in all the world
The sands and snow
The echoing oak
The peacock flow
Of ocean deep
The moon's fey show
While children sleep
The stoke of stars
The petal weep
Of summer's glow
In all the world
Beneath and on and through
The rarest joy is
You.

Nik Larcombe

THE MAN WITH THE BOMB

When the corner of a lip drooped,
and the right hand forgot how to write,
and a slur loosened the tongue,
and the alphabet was wiped from his brain
as if from a blackboard,
we knew then the bomb he carried.

Not at once, not until doctors had poked about -
named the white sheet that had descended
a stroke,
that pulled away like a tablecloth beneath
china cup and porcelain plate,
leaving a man rattling.

But that was not all of it -
once they had consulted their heavy tomes,
the ones riddled with long names in Latin,
then they could label the bomb -
endocarditus, disease of the blood,
one in a million.

Elegant fingers, surgical gloved,
opened his chest and found the pink muscle,
twitching as unpredictable
as dynamite. There they set a metal valve
to keep time - *tick-tock, tick-tock* -
regulator of the aorta.

They sewed him up, the long scar
a pale fuse, and gave him Warfarin
to ease through the thickened blood, and said
twenty years are now yours for the taking -
tick-tock, tick-tock - so go love your wife
and your children.

But the business of carrying bombs
is a dangerous one, a clock in a ribcage
marking off each second, a life lived
as though the present tasted sharp as lemon,
all too tart and vivid,
tipped on the edge of an explosion.
when he fell to the pavement-
dive years over the limit they had given -

he smiled, knowing what a cheat
a heart could be, hearing the sure pop
as he gathered his life about him -
back into the cavern of his open chest.

P Viktor

CADBURY FORT

A man-made fort lost to time,
With rings and ditches of clay and lime;
A tribal fort, a hilltop fort,
Durotriges ran, for king and clan
Till Rome came,
With sword and slain,
With shields raised high,
Death was their cry,
The last stand came,
On those windswept plains,
War gods were called
Modocie of war the mead sweet lord, to Mars,
God of war and death he roared.
The battle did rage with stone spear and sword,
Till the sun's last call and the shadows took its hoard,
For when the siege was done, Rome had won,
With victorious cries, they left the dead as one.
Many a year has passed since that day was done,
Times and mist have blended, the warriors as one,
But still to this day, the silent stare into the sun
For that is their home till the last shadows come.

Gregory McDowell

SOMETHING EASY/EXCRUCIATING

A hope divides what fate decides,
    Actions that formed a decision,
It relies on what we emphasise:
    A joining that caused an incision,
And all the while we reconcile -
    You made my sweat now yours,
Choose to mend, what we can't comprehend
    And I made you my new lost cause
Does not exist, what I can't resist
    The heat, the wetness and this grit,
A siphon of guilt; a tie that's built
    Rubs raw, yet still I'm drawn to it.
Of these broken words, sayings unheard,
    You don't think, not when you perform,
A perfect mass, cheapened, crass
    That all this pleasure is now forlorn.
This wasted smoke, too blackened to choke,
    Because all I love, I always forsake,
For now you're unaware, the easy is unfair
    And in favour of vanity, we fake.

Zoe Burke

SANCTUARY

This is my place,
In which to hide
And shield myself
From those outside.
No matter the day
My shoulder carry,
I turn to you
My sanctuary.

Marcus Tyler

ALL WINDOWS

From a great height glass amplified your dorsal,
being cornered at that point was pure chance,
in a plastic bag the spiny pews were cold
and everything was initially sterile,
life for you turned green, then black, then old, then
in time my own skin paled and then darkened, it rolled

my whims against a daft background, it was
me with that cheap ornamental ship, The Golden Hind.
Now, toned backs and dresses, artificially distanced began
whipping red back and forth, odd groans saw
exposed brick, monocles, bones, broad loans,
yeah, yeah, yeah, never again, sticky, sticky, but

through my window the ocean slumped down and
the trees that shot up like geysers from the Earth
peeled back cliffs so fossils could gaze forever at tall
church spires clung like ruined watchtowers with humble innards
about grounds where numbers fell and stone slabs fall,
separated by time and universal pains, I think that glass distorted us all.

Terence McCourt

SNOWDROPS IN MANCHESTER

First signs of spring when I first met Vicky on a March
Friday night outside Oxford Rd Station.

We grooved the local pubs
The Irish bar we gyrated to Kyle republican tunes.

In the Marlbora rocked to Led Zeppelin
Telling her my history of painting portraits
Writing poetry to life and Guinness.

She was clothed in snowdrops
Eternal white
Outlook on existence the same
Lifting the black dog from my shoulders.

The sun does shine in Manchester after all.

Alan Doherty

THE BIRD AND THE BUFFALO

The inevitability of death. Of all things in life,
this is most certain. A creature, once vibrant,
soaring the sky, its wings splendidly open
only concerned with the next meal.
Now a hollow feathered shell, discarded.
Feathers once shiny, are dull and flat,
ravaged by the forces of nature - snow, wind,
rain. Its significance in the world, forgotten.
Passers-by view its carcass, disgusted,
maybe amused. Someone with a tender soul
is struck by the sight of it, contemplates too
much about this bird, lonely in its death.
But alive and well is the buffalo, unaware of the
bird's plight, and the thin line that exists between
them. Today it stands curiously watching you
capture its image, weighing your intentions.
Tomorrow, next week, you return with your
camera, only to find an inanimate object, with
matted fur and absent eyes. When you have
youth, death is a myth. Age breeds mortal
thoughts. The need to feel, to experience the
extraordinary, becomes urgent. The birth of life
is as much of a guarantee as death. While today,
you are the buffalo, one day you will be the bird.

Tricia Morgan

BEECHING

The trains no longer run through here;
The glory days are past and gone.
The rails are silent, red with rust;
Deserted when the world moved on.

Where once a mighty loco stood;
A gleaming monster, snorting steam,
Mice and rabbits scamper now;
A pheasant dreams a summer dream.

The station's little garden plot,
Once carefully tended, rank with weeds;
A sad reminder of a faded past,
But no one sees it, no one heeds.

The ticket window's open ear
Hears no request for day returns,
Nor overhears a passing joke
Or someone's whispered deep concerns.

The platform, deathly silent now
Was once alive with busy noise
From men and women, young and old,
And small irreverent young boys.

The clock is stopped at half-past four;
The time the last train rattled by
And all is silent as the grave
Beneath the burning summer sky.

Richard Young

MASTERPIECE OF CREATION

A block of blue extends across the canvas;
With a sweep appear wisps of white.
A patchwork of green unfolds,
To reveal rolling hills and imposing mountains
Dotted with blobs of cotton wool.

Smudges of reds, browns and yellows
Add an injection of colour to the green fabric
Before the dark, drab drape of winter descends.
Streams of light scatter from the daub of yellow,
Highlighting the magnificent painting before us.

A critical eye is needed to appreciate
The intricate stitches that interweave and thread together
This awesome, awe-inspiring tapestry -
Splashed with colour,
Splurged with light,
Showered with love,
It truly is a powerful, provocative piece of art.

Sarah Loane

BARELY BREATHING

Throwing coins in the fountain, releasing ripples playing on
the water's surface.
A wish joined with the two-faced circle maybe of a new life or
something smaller.
Life's dreams need to change or maybe you'll end it sooner rather
than later.
Nothing ever turns out the way we plan so why bother.
Every day birds spreading their wings are flying the nest
Leaving a large hole in our universe.
Believing that it will get better, is something placed in our memory
By the elders of this world.
Hope has to be reality because the other choice is never talked about
Falling is not optional, reasons behind events don't matter
The shadows overcast it all, here is not living, here is dying.

Dylan Halliwell

SEE MRS WEST

See, Mrs West
Out here on your doorstep
One slightly used daughter
Returned with regret.
That isn't to say
He misused or abused her,
Despite all his caring
They just fell apart.
Their problems began
When he lost his work
And then he lost his way
And she followed him there.
Neither was stronger
So as each one faltered
Like fruit on the vine
They just softened and soured.
Each step they took
Was slower and harder,
They stumbled and tumbled
And fumbled their way.
Then one couldn't see
And one couldn't listen
And neither could talk,
Then they noticed one day.
At night, in the dark
They shared tender exchanges,
The world was at war on
Their small TV screen.
She cried as she watched
As the street bombs exploded;
How dare we desire -
How dare we to dream!
So, see Mrs West
Out here on your doorstep
One slightly used daughter
Returned with regret.
That isn't to say
He misused or abused her,
Despite all his caring
They just fell apart.

Patrisha Reece-Davies

OOPS . . .

I wonder what it would feel like to drown
To be that depressed that I'd want to die
What event would be big enough to push me over the edge
To commit my final act?
Maybe I should try the first step
What I call 'self harming'
So many people I know do this, why I do not know?
I could guess; attention seeking? Suffering abuse?
How would I know? Why would I want to?
Yet maybe there's something magical about the blade
Upon the skin.
When the flesh is cut and the blood rushes to the surface,
Something in that instance, a thrill, a release
Looking at it, watching.
You have to watch, to embrace the feeling or miss the magic.
It does not last long.
Each time you have to cut deeper, further, more,
Once you've felt the buzz, the thrill
You get addicted, wanting more and more
Until the blood looks so red against the skin,
Which is quite pale now.
Now I think about it, I've never seen myself whiter.
Just one more cut, one more thrill, one more
Buzz, one more release . . . then I'll stop.

Oops . . .

Esther Wilkinson (16)

THE GRANDFATHER CLOCK

The chiming of the clock
Broke the silence of the day
As the hands moved slowly round
If the clock should stop
Would time stand still too
And change my life forever
I felt angry with the clock
As it ticked away
Never realising how noisy it was
As I walked through the house
And into every room I could
Hear the sound of the clock
The grandfather clock which had stood in the hall
Since I had been a child
Will probably be there when my children grow up
Still ticking away
With each pendulum swing.

Doreen Cawley

HISTORY

Tears from the past
Creating paths of blood and loss
Ancient cries, arising from the bottom of the sea
Blood-coloured waters, how can all this be?

An illusion

Empty eyes
Dead bodies, swimming in the ocean
The ocean of His story
Where white ancestors sold his sisters
Bought by a grandfather, who cold-heartedly raped his mother
Screams trapped in time from a young murdered brother
Tears from the past
Carried by the wind as a remembrance of how it used to be
Voices of lost souls finally echoing free.

Linda Lundh

THE 213 BUS

Is busy with boys
tuning us *roll-up roll-up* skirted girls
into their guarded world with the share
of half a headphone.

Sherbet-sticky shouts reach up
and out to the dented steel above
to the steamy scratched windows
thrown next to your cheek.

I look at your feet, safe
Under the seat in the thick rubber soles, shifting
in their clumsy, quick-tied laces -
an uncomfortable bow.

You push the button for the bell
And we all know it's your stop.
Nut-heavy Snicker wrappers surf past your ear
rusty pennies print the Queen onto your head -

Held high, you never said goodbye.

Sabrina Mahfouz

UNTITLED

As he watched
The ocean hammered
On the forest floor
Footsteps in the rain

As they listened
Whispers through the leaves
A sudden emptiness, gone
Footsteps in the rain.

Corrine Davidson

COAL DUST STREET

And he saw it now and then
the lamp lit row of houses that
stretched beyond the eye
houses where men who dug black
slept and drank when they could

ageless cobbles pried on
men who fought in the street
over want, women and work
while little men sons played
foolish games of childhood

daughter women with prams
mothered their plastic dolls
and the wives gossiped about
young Sally who had a belly
by John Stout the butcher boy

the Reverend Ellis knew
all the stories and chapters
of life in this coal dust street
he birthed them, baptised them
married and buried them

and the street was quiet
no vehement voices tonight
as the deed of death
slipped over the cobbles
and gripped a sleeping soul.

George Carle

WALKING IS . . .

Breathing, seeing . . .
And the feeling of travelling . . .
Walking is . . .
Healing those that don't think clear enough . . .
Walking is . . .
Health if you don't drag your limbs with a limp
Walking is . . .
Not for the dead

As I step through my journey
Moving too fast and thinking to slow
Towards any direction that matters
There is more darkness on my path than shadows,
Traced no silver pavements and grazes the walls in its presence
I'm blind and photogenic,
Without a moment to suspend,
I'm one who needs to be reminded where his life went . . .

I'm this runaway that can't wait to slow down, but
Why slow down when the question isn't running through me?
Like water when I'm thirsty . . .
My dad is seventy, repeating the same songs
From the only youth he had,
He says time is like sand, the harder you grip the faster it falls
                              through your hands,
He won't be alive by the time I understand.

'Slow down,' he says
'You must slow down, absorb all you surround, it's the travelling
                              that matters'
I fail to appreciate just how much time he's had to think.
I slag him off because he gambles, he smokes and he drinks,
I raise my voice, point my finger and call him a hypocrite,
He never replies . . . and never denies the traits he's fitted with,
Years after this incident he'll look me in the eye. . .
Somehow I'll teleport back to this time . . .
Expecting a defence he doesn't deliver
. . . He says, 'There's too much to consider, to ever live like me'
And I still tell him he walks too slowly . . .

Ray Antrobus

INTERPRETATIONS

I am sure there will be some sentiments, about love, all that is, but I'm not feeling. They say poetry is dancing words then what is this? Poetry is smoke, light, elusive and mesmerisingly beautiful. True poetry is one of the few things that is certainly incorruptible. It is a constant that cannot be changed, twisted and used. Which is ironic as this is precisely what poetry is a corruption and twist, of prose. A contradiction in a world of hypocrites. Oh but what beautiful contradiction, sweet corruption. Sweet.

Picture,
The butterfly with pale delicate blue powdery wings, firing from flower to flower, the butterfly is poetry, fragile, beautiful and constant, now notice how the flowers are unique, as the butterfly touches them, they either embrace it. Offering up different interpretations, or they attempt to crush it, denying any feeling, the desire to be right, without thought to whether they qualify for this position or not, scientific contradictions. The flowers themselves are as different as their reactions to the butterfly, some are delicate and developed, others are far away, one or two are armoured and protected, they are decaying minds, the smell is rancid. All are flawed, as essentially as life itself, this is the human condition and without it, beauty and life cannot follow, be born and all is monotony, no feeling, just detached sex and drunkenness. Even the broken ones are beautiful.

Women are like butterflies giving with every essence of their being, every fibre, muscle, tendon, ligament and organ of their existence. Which is again ironic, as they feel that after the initial gift of life, they are done and now must take. Butterflies don't do this, they keep giving, again, again. Beautiful sounds, music and thoughts. Variation and dancing. Small grey tendrils offering an illusive majesty and gain, small blue butterfly wings disintegrate in the electric snap of the fly killer.

Lloyd Evans

THE POPPY

I am the colour of carnage,
Fuelled by deception,
Spawning courage,
Sacrifice yet salvation.
I am the colour of cruelty
And compassion,
Patriotism exploited by conflict
Into betrayal.
I am the colour of anger,
Whose legacy, fragile peace
Brings hope from despair,
Humanity from the edge of destruction.
I am the colour of sunrise
And sunset.
The beginning and the end
Of life.
Ultimately - I am the colour
Of remembrance
The tribute to and of freedom.

Janet Cullup

CHILDHOOD MEMORIES

Cornfields, roasted by the scorching sun,
Swaying in the southerly breeze,
Dotted with myriads of red poppies.

Cicadas, incessantly filling the quasi-tropical air
With their bold and raucous chants.

A distant horizon, traced by the emerald line
Of the tranquil waters of the Adriatic Sea.

Green pastures, coming to life with the bleating
Of newborn lambs in spring.

High mountains with white tops
Disappearing into stormy clouds in winter
And painted red by the sun going down in summer.

Anna Greaves

SIESTA

The city leans on harbour walls
And dreams. Waves leap and gleam
Then lap against the stones
Like fawning dogs. Yachts sway,
Rigging softly jigs pleading for attention.

On the balcony she sits enthroned,
Shadowed in a polygon of light,
Smoothes pages, glances down,
Smiles languidly as Nikos, parking,
Fails to dent his brother's wing.

The city's eyelids rattle down
And all subsides in silent heat.

The sun creeps round; its stealthy fingers
Brush her foot, her leg, her breast.

Some flies swoop down to catch her scent,
And try to paddle on her skin; she flicks,
They soar and swoop again.
She surrenders for a while
Then they repeat the game.

I watch from the shadows, too far away
To touch, but close enough to hear
Her breathe, to hear her sigh, to see
The billows in her hair stirred by the breeze.

She is complete, both stone and flesh,
Goddess and woman, not to be caressed
Or carved, beyond the artist's scope.
Reluctantly I tiptoe out to see
The still world come to life.

David Taylor

ARISE AND SHINE FOR EDUCATION

Arise and shine for education
Like day let us show light
Education, the window to open mind
Arise and shine for education.

With knowledge the light will shine and never go
Bringing wisdom, hope and success
Bringing bright future
Arise and shine for education

What do we learn and not gain in thee?
Education, the inspiration to success
Like a bright morning sun
Arise and shine for education

Like the sun showing light to the world
Let us show light in education
Like rivers let us flow in this belt of success
Arise and shine for education

Let us be mathematical
Multiply the hopes, knowledge and success
Divide our challenges and move on with education
Subtract the past and obstacles

But most of all let us be bigger than the sum of all parts
Encourage each other
To arise and shine
Arise and shine for education

Onward to all I say onward
We are the light of education
Let us glow and be seen
Arise and shine for education

Onward to all the people I say onward
For education is the gateway to success
If only we arise and shine
Arise and shine for education.

Blessing M Makande

JUST ONE MORE BITE

And swallow
And I've eaten all of my soul.
It was a bit tasteless, a bit bland,
It was mine after all.

I don't need it anymore -
Who needs a soul when they have curtains drawn
A single light
And coldness freezing all the way to bone?

I've said it before
But it never ceases to amaze me,
How I can be so
Alone
Yet my heart continues to beat.

It tells me I'm surviving
But am I living?
Without using it properly
My heart might shrivel up
And fade away.

If I could change something -
But then, this life is all I know.
Couldn't deal with too much light
What would I do with all the smiles?

So I just sit and stare at walls
They're blank and comforting.
I'm drawing to a conclusion
That I don't know anything.

Laura Birkin

IT'S BETTER TO TRAVEL THAN TO ARRIVE

I'm remembering that first time
That you took and held my hand
The way something jumped in my stomach
I couldn't quite understand
I'm remembering that first time
You gently brushed my hair from my face
It was a sign of your loving affection
Not that my hair was out of place
I'm remembering that first time
You looked lovingly into my eyes
Where your deepest emotions and feelings
And hurts and pain lies
I'm remembering that first time
That you turned up at my door unawares
When you hugged me right there on the step
Removing all worldly care
I'm remembering that first time
That you sat and ate a plate of food cooked by me
When you laid back on my sofa
So that you could simply be
I'm remembering that first time
That I began to realise I loved you
But even more beautiful to me
Is how much you love me too
I'm remembering that first time
When your fingers lightly touched my waist
Every ecstatic and wholesome feeling
My body, mind and spirit could taste
I'm remembering that first time
When you laughed out youthfully
Not held back by what I might think
If you did so in front of me
I'm remembering that first time
That your breath felt warm against my face
So I'm gonna contentedly do this journey
Instead of running the race
Because after all
It's better to travel than to arrive

And to savour and bask in
The way when I'm with you I come alive
Yes it's far better
To travel
Than to arrive.

Michelle Campbell

I DON'T DO POETRY

The cliché of modern verse
Language licked to
Contradict
The writer's curse

Which stops to reason
To stop the treason
Of time.
It jolts in the throat
But it swims in the mind

The meter grows faster
To meet her still after
I kill it in bloom

To savour the bitter taste
Of knowing I can
But it stops for no man

Waits for no fool
Is money
Of the essence
And Father, stitching his nine
Is laughing at me
Not laughing at her
But staring at him

I don't do poetry
I don't do love

Matt Crow

THE GOODBYE KISS

He kissed her
On the forehead
On the cheeks
She hugged him hard
Could not let go
Kept holding onto him
Tears filling their eyes
'Do not go,' she said
I have to
'But you will leave me'
There are more important things to be
I will always be there
By your side
Just do not forget
They departed
Both crying
Just as soon as
She turned her back
He disappeared
Left to his fate
And in a blink
A shot was heard
A mother was killed
With her children around
Her son has just left to join the defence
Someone said
And he gave her
A goodbye kiss
They both died
But just as he said
They are always there
Alive
Watching in despair
Mourning over us
Not us over them
A story
Of a goodbye kiss

That we all miss
That we all crave for from Palestine
In our hearts
They lie within.

Yassmin Elnazer

THE CUCKOO'S CALL

The cuckoo's sweet serenade
Echoes everywhere this summer day
Perfidious, polygamous, promiscuous
They call you this not without reason
Despite your sweet soliloquy
You are a treacherous bird
Deceiving crows, ugly scavengers
Laying eggs in their naïve nests.

But I love your cadences
Echoing over the hills
Rising symphonic in the sky
In harmonious melodies
In summer's stifling heat
When sweat pours and
The mind seeks respite.

Cuckoo, you sweet siren
The elusive sylph
Ephemeral wanderer of the forests
If you deceive the crow and fly away
Would your children caw like the crow?
Or sing the traitorly song of summer
In the valley of our habitation?

John P Matthew

THE CRYING MONA LISA

She smiled hiding the tears
That tore her heart with spears
Her concepts not yet articulate
At thirteen her menstruation late
Her baby-like groans destitution
In the raping blade of deception
At the very place called home
Abuse under the loving dome
Molestation denied in the paedophile dark
Forbidden to pay in the observant park
Her face with unpromising smiles
As her eyes with tears of piles
Look deep on the parental hands
That refused protection that mends

She smiled

In the streets of Johannesburg
Where she had to beg
Searching for shelter in brothels
Conforming, her love no longer petals
No more, does or does not
Petulant in the throbbing of stranglers
Euphoric in the monetary palace
With amnesia to please
In a spell of white diamonds
Her life, dry like forgotten ponds
Descending into the undefined files
When her life had been nothing but miles
Now as afar as the scarecrows on poles

She smiled

Sited on the vestiges of splendour
When she thinks of anything but pleasure
How her existence inclined in terror
When she hoped to expunge horror
In the palms of a chauvinistic fool
His alcoholic tummy full
Careless on her fragile body
As he trains on her, in her monody

Pleading forgiveness of tragedy
When you cannot tell if she's a lady
His sober sobs scripted
In an act indecently opted
When she did not the words heed
That told of this man's need

She smiled hiding the tears
That tore her heart with spears
Her sorrow lamented in prose
Telling her eloquent ache in poise
Her feminine uniqueness regal
How touching her is illegal
When she yells for assistance
To obliterate the ghosts of hate
Forced on a sexist plate
By this boy who called himself
Her man

She smiled
In her estuarial radiance
Told by Da Vinci in prose.

Linda Sakazi Thwala

BAG LADY

Sitting at restaurant tables
Devoid of food - just aching feet
And a need to rest.
Hoping no one will chase her away.
Streetwalker, household goods
And memories in a plastic bag
Like so much twenty-first century
Rubbish.

Janet Mary Zylstra

EMERGING

Fighting to see the light
500 feet under
Crawling, climbing up
Is that a glimmer?

No, the journey continues

Being pushed down
How did I get there?
Struggling, gasping, heaviness
Every stone of the way

Tons of filth you force upon me
Making me feel dirty and trapped
If only I can push through

Realisation kicks in
The dirt I feel is not true
I am not trapped
I am free

I am free.

Danielle Miller

LOVE AND LAUGHTER

(For Stef)

When you hear laughter,
Remember my name,
Save it to your mind,
Sneak like a child
To your secret den.
Open that thought
Like an old faded love letter,
Remember, please remember
The laughter, and how much
Just how much, I love you.

Denny Denwood

PALM SUNDAY

Another day,
Another load,
Another shekel.
Burden a beast,
Beast of burden,

Poor asinine fool!

Another ache,
Another toil,
Another struggle.
Unyielding my life.
Poor asinine fool!

Another dream,
Another hope,
Another fantasy,
Blistered and broken,
Broken, destroyed.
Poor asinine fool!

Why then,
This fire in my belly?
Why then,
The heady sweetness of dates
Pervading my senses?
Am I the bearer
Or is he?
My burden lighter,
Lighter my spirits.

Another day,
Another lifetime,
Another promise.
Tawdry and battered,
Battered and bruised.

Poor asinine fool!

No!
Ears pricked,
Head raised n triumph.
Heart and soul of
A Nemean lion.
Hallelujah!

Eileen Real

BESOTTED WITH A MONSTER

Jekyll and Hyde, our hearts collide, your love is like a cancer,
It grows inside, where it resides, not wanted or sought after.

Here lies a human paradox with two faces and two minds,
Locked in a narrow shallow box with your beauty unrefined.
A stranger in my nightmare with a constant echoing voice,
I got a feeling sinking in me that's not rid by will or choice.

I need a second chance, a second coat of bright white paint,
This is an obscure case of two fiends wrapped up in restraints.
With misanthropic tendencies, shadowing our human decency,
These demons wanting to be free, with no safeguard guarantee.

It's time for you to let go and shift the blame to me,
We've lost our minds, all that's left is rind, from an old and rotting tree.
For you I took away your monster, the person you despise,
Now I am both our monsters and this girl is my disguise.

Dear Jekyll, I'm Hyde, now we divide,
This sickness continues to metastasise in me.

Josephine Dickinson

BRIGHTON

This is November in Brighton:
Leaden tides strain and groan,
Cough spume onto
Shivering beaches
As the wind,
With frosted breath,
Shouts out its salty warnings
Along the pebble-dashed promenade.

Brian Hays

TRAIN JOURNEY

I sit on the train staring out of the window
I see a mum embracing her beautiful daughter
Who is getting on the train
The daughter looks out at her mum standing there
She waves with the most magic of smiles on her face
A tear trickles down her mother's face
She turns slightly so her daughter cannot see her pained lined face
As she brushes it away
Hiding it with a look of love
For her beautiful daughter who is moving on
She turns her head with sadness in her eyes
She knows she has to let go
But it's hard as they have been together so long
There will be an enormous gap in her life
But she smiles a smile of reassurance
For her beautiful daughter who needs to be free
I sit on the train as my eyes brim with tears
I blink them away
As the train pulls away from the station
I look back and still see the mum waving in the distance.

Lynne Whitehouse

AS ONE

Blissfully I embrace you my prodigious husband,
My sublime love for your soul infused into mine intoxicates me,
Yielding me into total delectation.
Our hearts pound en masse and our breath concurrent,
Intuitively, conceding your powerful constitution,
Crying out in complete beatitude.

Anne Plaggenborg

233

BETWEEN WAKING AND DREAMS

Twilight and nobody

Here, almost as if
We forgot,

Or God
Forgot,

Letting the Earth
Roll, boil the whole
Day, licked by lava
And suddenly thinking to let
One worm ooze
Loose from mud . . .

Then
A thump as the first creature
Tightens its almost-belly.

The legs
Of the insects; listen.

Nobody.

Just the first
Flower breaking open
One hour before
Midnight.

A ring-tailed lemur
Spilling its musk slowly
Into deep grooves of bark.

Now a noble Celtic princess,
Watches her dark daughter
Stripping silk from corn
In the shade.

In just a few
Minutes she will finish
She talks, then sleeps
Deep in those woods.

The bones
Of her hands will be buried
Under an oak and dug up
There,

In my childhood,
Reaching out to me. . .

Between waking and dreams.

David R Morgan

THE TUNNEL

In life's dark tunnel
Blindly we grope our way
Towards an unseen goal.
Our outstretched hands
Touch objects that remain half known,
Half guessed,
And all around us are the cold, strong walls
That close us in.

Yet in the walls are cunning mirrors built
With faces that reflect a world
Of changing beauty, wonderful to see.
And all our lives are spent
In searching for the best
Amongst the differing views.

But should our lunging hands
Stray in desire to touch these sights,
Then singing rays lash out
To punish us for our presumption.
And into deeper darkness are we thrust.
And sorrowing
Forced to go upon our way.

Stephen Parry

I WAS THE ONE

I was the one who loved you,
Because I smiled when you did me wrong,
I was the one who loved you,
Because I think of you in every song,
I was the one who loved you,
Because I remember all the little things,
Like you stroking my hair,
Waking up and you're there,
Watching your heart go through growth and repair.

I was the one who loved you,
Because no one could compare,
I was the one who loved you,
When she hurt you I cared and all your pain, I shared,
I was the one who loved you,
Because I had faith in you when yours disappeared,
I was the one who loved you,
Because I lent you my ear and let you share your deepest fear,
I was the one who loved you,
For everything you're not and for all that you are,
I was the one who loved you,
Because I let you into me,
I was the one who loved you,
Because I had these words to write poetry,
I was the one who loved you,
Because I can let you be happy and walk away from me,
I was the one who loved you,
Because I knew I'd love you better, but she had your heart and I let her.
The nicest words you said you'd heard,
Were 'I Love You,'
Sometimes you don't need to hear it,
Just know the feelings true,
Those words I never said,
You should have seen them between the lines you read.

Starlena McKetty-Campbell

SHARING IN THE MEMORIES OF MY LOVER

I am invited as a bare witness
To her unpacking of certain things.

They are wrapped so artfully,
So perfectly,
And always so necessarily.

Each is bound tight by barbed wire and a child's bright ribbon.
Heir tight seals prevent any unplanned inheritance.

In my vulgar haste to be involved,
I lurch into trying
To help you to open one.

Now my ego is bleeding; I have not the skill nor grace.
These are not my boxes.

So I return to watching you.
Perform your self constructed rituals,
These are your only traditions.

What will you show and tell today?
Which window will we go through?

Will you dress me up in a ghost's smile, dredged up from your own past
sunshine?
Will I be a child again, indignant and waving that plastic sword?
Red cheeked and chasing the dragon's tail of your former pains?

I trust you.

I trust your choice of which boxes to share by opening
And which to share by leaving.

Allen Bailey

THE PROFITEER

Aye! My people
In this time of empty
We have sold plenty
Just for a little
Now is our time
To sell few for dime.

In the wake of the summer
Assuming riches from exotic profit
Building castle in the city
Gallivanting town in a hummer
Losing all to storm whip
As the winter goes to sleep.

The profiteer never compromise
Till the hour came knocking
As the Jericho wall falling
The borrower never compromise
Like the proverbial python
Glued to the crimson.

Profiteer do penance for humour
Even if it will be a rumour.

Aina Oladipupo Abiodun

UNTITLED

I want to be famous . . .
I want to footspin the world
Into a web of stars
Dream on Jupiter and dine on Mars
Be the cocktail in Heavenly bars
See my words effervesce
As the vapours of inspiration
Nobody have the doubt to say they're Oscar Wilde's
But the certainty to say they're mine.

Michele Cavannah

A SOLDIER'S DREAM

I was there at the battleground
As soldiers of the black army
Marched forward in battalions
And the red ants in camouflage
Laid ambush in decayed leaves.

To fight for my country I was bought
Like Hercules of Greek legend
And in all the wars that I have fought,
Men have kissed their untimely end.

Yesterday I saw in a dream
The death of a brave soldier
Writhing with pains in his bloody stream
Blast to shreds by a bombardier.

Beware soldier the dice of fate
For whether it be on sea or land
Death has more than just a gate
And for you may make one brand.

When I fly above war fields
And ground soldiers to battle roar,
I see the dead with swords and shields
Sing and chant their songs of war.

When I think how old Troy fell
Though it had brave Hector,
Fear so great I cannot tell
Pins my heart in the raptor.

The gods of war have fled at last
And ghosts have come to fight with men.
Though my guns rattle and blast,
I am afraid I know not when.

When I think of Hector brave
That thrusts his sword and paints it red
I see from above a lonely grave
And in it an empty bed.

For I was there at my funeral
And for all the wars that I have fought,
Life is but ephemeral
And death at last a soul has caught.

Paul Oche

MEN AND POWER

How readily men on heat descend into the bottomless pit
To rape and kill their brothers' wives and children; the shame of it,
When given power; just a bit.
When given power over death and life,
He, this man, turns his eager hand to caress with care
A well oiled gun or fine honed knife
And then forgets that he, in some distant place,
Has also a child like them
And like them, a wife.
Yet no need at all, to justify this manly urge to kill,
A rationale of primeval fathers and born in lust with blood to spill
And ever insatiable and never once achieves its fill.
He orders them with trembling hands to scrape in earth,
A shallow hole,
In fear, to kneel with hands tied firm,
Assuming then that assassin's role
And there, as Cain, beneath the innocents he kills,
He buries deep his own soul
As Faustus did, though merely to portray some truth in dramatic effect lest an
observing audience miss that little bit
And if God looks down, if God can, as some say, know,
The shame of it is that He doesn't show the love that they say
Fills His eternal heart
As they in a pointless, painful abandon, from the life
He gives them, depart
And if it's true that his inaction is the worthy price of Man's freewill
Then let His prophets explain away the grief
To the mothers of the slain
And the tortured and the raped
That the price for choice in pain is well worth it
In a city; Nanking,
And a village; Mi Lau,
In a sea port; Salé
In a camp; Dachau,
In a field in Armenia
Or in the Cambodian rain,
In the hills of Croatia
On Rwanda's great plain
Or on the back streets of Bazra
Or in some Lebanese cell
Where the innocents suffer

In this practice for Hell
And now it's in Mumbai
Where blood is released,
Where more innocents die
And the murder's not ceased
And hardly ever, the question;
How? Or why? Or where? Or what's it for?
The gates of Hades with a well greased door
Hinges open with one-fingered ease
And then much too late to fall down on our knees
But enter that place
Where souls are forfeit by men on heat,
Eternal in regret
And the Devil shrugs in embarrassment
And wonders at the ease of it.

Henry Stewart

SILENT WAR

Battlefield.
Sounds of gunfire
Rock the victory floor.
Blackened muskets burning
And red blood
Showers three hundred soldiers.

Black crows dressed in mourning
Drink the silence of dismembered men,
The river doesn't ripple
Nor the trumpet sound again,
Only a mist of memories
Quells the horses' thundering hooves.
Their spirits now lie wasted
In this eerie woodland den.

As we listen quietly
We don't hear the battle cry,
Or the rustle of the leaves,
Or a soldier passing by.

Mary Mullett

DESTRUCTION

In darkened shadows we move, over oceans we sail
High atop mountains, a thousand miles underground
We love, then lose, then love again
Never precisely defined, holding only the night as our friend
And only substances are our guiding hands, with icy fingertips that
                                        trace our spines
And sharpened, feminine nails that scratch the skin of our backs
Through night we ride a wave of love and sex and music and zen
Whilst Dionysus casts his seductive hand over the heads of many
And scatters their remnants across the caliginous sky
And through day we are swallowed by Horus' divine retribution

Alas, Hephaestus, with such wit and jocoseness
I sit awake at night and mourn the times we never shared
For our paths crossed only briefly, and we drifted apart
But though neither of us knew it, you were the most perfect friend
                                        I ever had
And though we both felt Dionysus' hand on our shoulder
You were but a flicker on the horizon before I was under his spell
Whilst you had long since become embroiled in a web of substance
                                        and violence
Perhaps Dionysus' doing, perhaps someone else's
Perhaps your own, it is irrelevant
You left me standing alone, with only solitude for company
The last of the cliff to crumble into the sea

And in the time I needed her most, Aphrodite came to return me my sanity
Her truth and divinity enamoured me, her impermanence almost as
Unfathomable as her loveliness
For only until the fourth month would she remain, and I could Scarcely see life
beyond her
Every day she laid her arms around me, and echoes of her voice Reverberated
around my skull
And when Dionysus' act with a French girl was revealed
And I was left drowning in a sea of mental anguish
The sound of her voice, the feel of her skin on mine,
Was enough to bring me to calmer waters.

Jake Allport

LIFE PARTNER

You know in an instant when you meet him
That you've found your love,
Your life partner, your true match.

You see a reflection of your inner-self within him,
In the dreams you share, the expectations and morals you uphold.

But over time, stresses from the outside world
Taint the values of your partnership,
And you lose sight of your purpose together . . .

Regardless, you strive on but notice a feeling within you,
And a change in the connection between you both.
Then, you discover that he has lost his way,
And breaks your heart . . .

A feeling of sickness and heart-stopping panic surges through your body;
A sense of total disbelief overwhelms you,
When your heart is broken and you hurt all over;

The world as you know it becomes polluted with distrust,
The way you perceive people becomes distorted with questions of doubt.

Slowly, you heal through the immeasurable pain of deception,
Beginning to trust yourself, to trust again,
To trust him to be open in your relations, keeping no secrets;
For him to be honest about everything.

And now you realise,
That the only guarantees in life are the ones you make for yourself,
And in reality,
You never get to truly know anyone, except yourself.

Be true to yourself.

Amanda Philipe-Savage

ARE PEOPLE BODIES?

In the little glowing box
Where they shrink your head
They've removed the couch
And wheeled in the dissecting table
Antiseptic as a reductionist altar
Where they open people up
On the cop shows, on the op shows
Where they slice the skin asunder
Reach inside among the organs
And find not love nor soul
But unusual stomach contents
Where drugs are suspect
It's a church of faith denied
In the ecclesiastic hush of pathology
Where the ministers are women
Barren and vulnerable and lost
Sterile in this environment
Constructing their intimate victims
Into bodies in the post-fatal
Embrace of the autopsy
Priestesses of unfulfilment
Daughters of sublimated desire
Witness Scully
Witness Silent Witness
Women of a certain age
Of contingent lives
Hungry eyes
And probing scalpels
Ripping apart their victims
Tearing out their hearts
To be mummified
In formaldehy
Between the fleshback sequences
Of the life that's left behind
The little tragedy that's ended thus
Vignettes of roles now pointless
While the Greek cop-chorus moralise
Sons and lovers
A reluctant traitor
A corrupt industrialist
His once-handsome features

Viewed for the final time
Before the grim lady in the white coat
Tears off his face
But of course there's nothing there
But the deathmask grin of time
And the stifled whiff of atrocity
And this is the real pornography
As the screen drips red
And the brain is weighed
Within its aluminium bowl
In a rite where hope is gone
And the heroine's forlorn
And there's no room
For the soul.

Mark Madden

TO THOSE WE LEFT BEHIND

Happy we 'pals' of battalions, from villages borne of love
And sweet tender mercies; unlike here entrenched
With the foe, grey mists on the horizon, silhouetted hove
Of sallow composition; subdued and drenched.

Between us, in 'no-man's-land', a barren waste
Of limbs stacked high, orchestrating the way
Of death, foreshadowing yet even still the taste
To come, and soon; at the break of day.

Our friends, our fathers, uncles and brothers
In arms; cleaving the ground of crimson red
Left on the battle scarred plains, with their mothers'
Voices ringing out; as bells that toll the dead.

Then slowly feint whispers are heard amidst the grave
Of brown and grey; 'Is that you John! Bill! Fred!'
'Is that you Jurgen! Rommel!' Hans! you the brave
Who fell, still living amongst the dead.

The shroud of death that covers distempered cries,
Now lifting as 'both' find their heroes of 'cause';
And naked transgression remains; signature of lies
And deceit; like whores, showing no remorse.

Edward J Clark

BIRTHDAY BLESSINGS

Big bouncy bubbly
Birthday blessings
Burst in on me today
Like outsized balloons.
If I climb inside one
Will I be safe from sadness
Pain and anguish?
Maybe, for a while - but think how bored I'd be!
I'll opt for life's usual mix,
Its growth-inducing cocktail of
Blessings and blastings
Joys and jiltings
Successes and sorrows
Frustration and frivolity
Disappointment and delight- that's what I'm used to.
So birthday blessings, stay a day
Then float away
Until I need you next!

Stella Durand

WAR WITHOUT END

Throughout our history there has been strife.
A cull of youth, through unremitting wars.
Struck down still in the very prime of life.
Through leadership, bereft of all remorse.
Humanity is such, there's always greed
For power, wealth, resources some have got.
But others not, yet crucial is their need.
So they must have it all, or share the pot!
Now think of other leaders, who, in fear,
Defend themselves against the stronger might
Of super powers resolved to domineer.
Regardless of whoever's in the right!
Add dogma and belief which never cease,
To know the world will never be at peace.

Christopher Head

CAUGHT ON CAMERA

Caught on camera, her eyes so bright,
I looked at this poor mite,
Her belly swollen, her feet all sore,
What did she know of this war?

Days and nights spent in the dust
Who if anyone could she trust,
Looking for food, a small bowl,
Not enough to fill that hole.

Her mother's warm arms to sleep,
All she can do is weep,
No toys to play with, no Santa Claus,
Surely we should stop and pause.

They are innocent unprotected,
How would we feel if we were rejected,
Caught on camera, her eyes so bright,
I looked at this poor mite.

Mo

UNTITLED

A whiff of Jeyes Fluid,
Hair like thistledown,
Out with the hoards
And hunters.
Red cheeked
From too much money,
And too much money
To have any free time.
The opposite of liberation
Pauses on hilltop,
Casts an eye,
And wonders
What her husband
Of twenty-five years
Actually does
For a living.

Paul Schofield

WOE IS TINSLEY (OPERETTA)

God 'elp us, t'yard's bin shut down
Le nostre famiglie certamente starve
(our families will surely starve)
We ain't got no more skills
Sediamo appena nel paese catena-furnare
(We just sit at home chain-smoking)
Tab after tab after tab
Woe is Tinsley
Woe is Tinsley

Since Maggie t'unions 'ave gone
Hanno detto che hanno rovinato l'industria della Gran-Bretagna
(They said they ruined Britain's industry)
We ain't go no more steel
La depressione sta arruginendo le nostre vite
(Depression is blighting our lives)
Day after week after year
Woe is Tinsley
Woe is Tinsley.

We fight us mates at t'club
L'emozione frustrata funziona su
(Frustrated emotion runs high)
T'government them say 'Learn new skills'
Gli uomini sviluppati piangono nella loro birra
(Grown men weep into their beer)
Pint after pint after pint
Woe is Tinsley
Woe is Tinsley

T'giros don't go nowhere like
Come li invitare a sopravvivere
(How do they expect us to survive)
Last night us all had bloody Oven Chips
Mentre le classi medie gorge su claret
(Whilst the middle classes gorge on claret)
Glass after bottle after vat
Woe is Tinsley
Woe is Tinsley.

Tim Smith

POEM FOR JESUS

Veronica bakes a cake for Jesus.
Mary washes his feet, with her hair,
With care.
He visits Martha's house,
For a little while . . .

On the whole, however,
He is happier with the boys,
His apostles.
Man's talk,
Wandering about
Impressing everyone
With earnestness and vision -
Larging it,
Putting it about,
Rounds in for everyone,
Wine and fish suppers . . .

We are all impressed.

Same as it ever was
The wonder of man
Men behaving goodly . . .

(I won't say
Look where that got him)

Caroline Kemp

OPERATE

You fix people without even trying
But still you can't understand yourself
You need chaos and confusion
Just so you can operate
Happiness is for the weak.

Ross Dryburgh

THE THREAD

Watch, stare, a delicate thread hangs mid-air,
The thing slightly swings under a constant glare of a lighted candle and twists,
coils and distorts, and dances there.
Silently, observe with naked eye a well-notched course o'er a dark
Glazed sky; thro' the jittering, glittering stars that spangle,
Where the delicate thread itself is dangled; before an unopened door the weaving
thread becomes complicated,
Ensnared, and even tangled - stop!
Surely are you not at home, in bed? Are these not just nightly vision dreams
unfolding within your head?

In shrouded breath, it draws its reviled menacing form, swimming thinly; poised
Like some ghastly animated, make-up feature; an abominable black shadow

creature -

Thro' that jaded night you swiftly take to flight; panting, running,
But the thing keeps coming - snapping - snorting; volatile forming, an insidious
writhing, demon-like serpentine raises its ugly head, opens its mouth and sets to
strike,
And smites the soul with one almighty, piercing, devouring bite . . .

You awake, your body trembles and shakes; your escape is great,
But no one foresees or explains the coming angst, the coming pain -
For that which is born spirit-free succumbs to the black shaped death;
Man's immortal enemy.

Fight - fight with all your strength and might, escape the Reaper's booming cape;
You're strong at will, shake off the ugly spectre's kill! You're not one to lie and die;
Don't languish as some foe vanquished, spit death in its abhorrent eye;
Laugh before its ugly face of vile -

Mind-body-spirit-strength equals souls-crushing-destructive-denial . . .

Pills for this - pills for that; those that keep vigil offer up a silent prayer or two
A thread of hope; a cure of wonder, even a last minute miracle will do.
Long, strenuous weary haggles; desperate, never-ending, countless, poignant
battles -
Rest - gentle - rest; close your eyes to a myriad murmured sighs and ushered
silent cries;
And the path where cold-hearted wrath no longer treads - snips the thread . . .

Glenwyn Peter Evans

DRIP-DRIED IN A CUT-THROAT MANCUNIAN WIND

Theatrical crooning mixed with a rough trade of cocktails and romantic angst
Caught the eyes of the youth like a rabbit in the headlights
And the hand in the glove was pulling at the strings
And tugging in another direction as ambiquity advanced
Through the trancelike rhythms as if voodoo spells dancing through the mind
Of a disaffected youngster who took controversy and kicked it from behind.

It's dog eat dog and the overflowing opinions act as if they're clogged
In a society of bedsit blues, where one man stood ready with the guillotine
Ready to decapitate, the every word and all of the Iron Lady's views.
With a passion for flora in abundance and a luxuriance for Oscar Wilde,
The mystical knowledge of the blackness that James Dean had, was so sad
His world is yours . . . although it's temporarily beguiled.

So hold your breath and freeze the moment when Chernobyl cried
As the DJ spun his vinyl tracks, the anguished screamed,
Requesting that we hang him out to dry
But the newshounds typed and hyped the panic,
Sadness drip-dried in the cut-throat Mancunian wind
But to own a sense of melancholia, Mr Smith is not a Catholic sin.

You're not a Mother Theresa for the maladjusted,
Diamonds are not encrusted around abstract art.
Every day is not a Sunday but Monday's emeralds and sapphires
Inject euphoria into a bleeding heart.
So as you walk the long, uneven and cobbled pathways, don't look around,
But taste the afterglow of your Englishness upon your tongue
And let others feel the need to wear the Devil's caustic crown.

Let the Super Trouper shine amongst the darkened headlines
And the cyclorama cast its reflection of lily-white dreams
To move the ouija's planchette to spell your name amidst the bleak November
mists
And for the monster in the recess of your mind to muffle your uncle's screams,
Somewhere from Sunbury to Southampton the severed alliance can be locked
away
Madness can be reunited and sometimes the Southpaw will have his day.

And that day's the day where controversy reigns
And his tormented mind seeks out sanctuary until the time is right again
To write again, with words and music that squeeze the skull
Until the clouds of blackness form.
You were good in our time Mr Music, but Mr Morrissey has been reborn . . .

Alan Glendinning

251

THE WHITE SQUARE

The soldier was crying
When they took him out at dawn.
'Chin up lad,' said the sergeant,
'Take it like a man.'
But he was seventeen,
A frightened boy
When they found him
Cowering in that barn
While his friends were slaughtered
For their country.
He struggled as they tied him
To the post,
Pinned a white square above his heart,
Pulled a blindfold
Over his sad eyes.
'Keep still now!'
Ordered a voice,
Then - more gently -
'Soon be over.'
Soon be over:
Nightmares of battle,
Sounds from Hell,
The wretching and the terror,
A child lost forever.
Better the enemy bullet
Than this sudden volley
From five reluctant comrades.
Was there pain?
Did he shout for his mother?
And I would like to know:
What did those witnesses believe
When they saw my son
Slumped there
Suddenly silent,
Chin down -
Their dawn sacrifice.

Susan Cooke

EBB . . . TIDE

Synchronicity expounded
Resounding melodies
That permeate my mind space
Procreation of thought.
Word, sound, power
Advancing intellect
Burning neglect
Ions wavering . . . spacial
While conflicts rage.
Deemed racial
Who will contain the beat?
Does redemption reside in the east?
Too much stress in the west
Drive-bys and gang ties . . . many wet eyes.
Bombings in the east . . . Devil's feat.
Causes brought into concubinage.
Children murdered in a poor village
Totally unnecessary blood . . . spillage
I'm about to be sick
Can I just spit
About a corrupt word politick, emphasis on the tick . . . bloodsuckers
Arms dealers . . . death merchants . . . Swiss bank accounts
Do you count your dollars in blood?
Do your greenbacks bleed . . . do they cry out at night?
Does the acrid smell of charred rotting flesh tickle your nostrils?
Does the smoke get in your eyes?
Do visions of lifeless bodies haunt you as you sleep?
Lives sold cheap
Sowing the wind . . . Reaping the whirlwind
While publicists put a spin on sin.
Suddenly above the din a Rastaman chimed in
'Highly blessed' and bowed his head.
'Things are dread,' he said,
As we revel in war.
Who will fight for peace?
Who will fight for justice?
Somebody? Anybody?

Charles Matheson

WAITING

Mist from tunnel now clearing
Train coming into view
I stand on the platform
Waiting for you

Two years have passed
Since I waved you goodbye
To fight for King and country
Wiping tears from my eyes

In your smart army uniform
You made me so proud
Many others were boarding
But you stood out in the crowd

Letters and tokens
You sent from the front line
Proclaiming your love
And confirming you were mine

Would you remember our parting kiss
How have you changed after all this
Time can protect memories of you
Marriage vows taken honest and true

The mist now returning
Steam train pulling away
Crowds all dispersing
No more passengers today

The letter in my hand crumpled and old
Confirming the news which had to told
Over the top you went on that day
Silent and peaceful, on the battlefield you lay

I return to my home
Knowing you will not be there
I will always love you my brave darling
No one in future will ever compare.

Annie Hulbert

IDENTICAL TWINS

Like two peas from the very outside.
But inside we are not the same.
We love each other of course we do,
To be separated would be such a shame.

Just one egg was split in two,
Keep us close, keep us close, keep us close.

We were close entwined within the womb,
And our closeness grew and grew.
It was finally time to see the light,
It was time to see the blue.

It was getting far too cramped in there,
Give us space, give us space, give us space.

I heard a yell, a muffled sound,
My brother was out of sight,
But my neck was caught in a loving embrace,
With a cord that held me tight.

If I could just escape it,
Give me life, give me life, give me life.

From year to year as we grew up,
There was adventure, fun and laughter,
But now he has found a different mate,
And would go like lamb to the slaughter.

There was no escape, the hurt would come,
Give him love, give him love, give him love.

Years have passed, and we grew old,
We are withered, old, unsure.
We are gramps and grumps, and all such names,
Names we must endure.

We see the young and vitality,
Give us health, give us health, give us health.

We have lived, but, so far away,
And seventy years apart,
Not long to wait, to be together again,
These twins will soon depart.

If we could just receive it,
Give us peace, give us peace, give us peace.

Kenneth Anstiss

THE REMEMBRANCE OF SELF

The world can be a cruel place, a fierce and unforgiving tidal wave,
Washes of bad people all out to get you, pressures of living push down on us too.
Daily struggles of travelling to the nine to five,
Beating through red tape are a constant fight.
Everyone seems to be your finest critic; each honest move you make is up for stick.
Glued with harsh and constructive feedback, these mines of worry blast you off
track.

Then my remembrance of self happened one day,
As I walked through the city on my own little way,
My heavyweight frame came under unsavoury scrutiny
From a group of misfits and cap-wearing teens
'Hey fatso! Oi love! Did you eat all the pies?' the common accent and intent left
doubting tears in my eyes.
My mouth sealed, no retorts, could come, tongue gagged,
Their latest victim of comedy and bully triumph was bagged.
Left there on the pavement was the confident remnants of me,
Words ringing distaste in bones and all I could see.
I knew that I would be reeling from the blokey jokes for some time, revengeful
Karma buzzed in voodoo chants of mine.
Hands clenched in my pockets, my anger welled so deep,
This time their words I refused to keep.
So the left side of the brain kicked out at the right,
No negative minutes shall pass just positive hopes, I will hang on tight.
Rushes of compliments came thick and fast, a blanket of spoken comfort to
cradle my recent farce.
Old voices, ghostly mediums from beyond this time,
These were gems that helped to rescue my mind.
'You're a heavenly gift, my Botticelli, my girl, my every reason, and my best
destiny.'

Now the laughing faces disappeared without any of my care,
As I realised that all good things about me I must save and share.
So please remember yourself when others dare not,
Fist grab tightly at the received good memories you have got.

Keely Mills

DROWNING IN A STREAM OF CONSCIOUSNESS

Even when I'm happy I feel a certain kind of despair lurking
It never really goes away, depressingly depressed
And depressing, depressed's a word that weighs you down
To depress, to be crushed, to be struggling to breathe
Unable to help yourself, gasping, panicking
To panic
When you even hear the word
With the ultimate ironic insult, seeing your mother die from depression,
Feeling like there is no way out except death
To follow the path where the light is held
The only light that can ever erase the pain
Into the numbness and ecstasy of death
With a clarity that only death can bring through finality
The end of the physical state
And into the conscious being of the self
The mind existing outside itself
The internal confusion escapes and focuses without a focus
As I write a full stop attempts persuasion
Life is about working towards an end yet never reaching that end
Forever struggling towards death where we are told
It is not the end with life after death
That we can never 'know' as knowledge suggests the physical body
And now I feel exhausted and as tired as jealousy
In fact all emotions exhaust us and lead us into lethargy
Even happiness and excitement leave us a little worn
After the elation, no space to breathe a breath when reading aloud
Our nature provides a force that cannot take us into eternity . . .

Floating above an eternity where the eternal eternally forget
And nothing but nothing becomes nothingness.

Charlotte Grace Hopkins

THE TRUTH OF CHILDREN

A child
Free-thinking spirit
Own thoughts
Making own decisions and plans

Secretive, hiding
Industrious work

For someone always stuck
Like the plug in the sink
As the torrent hits
In the depth of darkness
A child, holding a drawing
Done for you
Saying, in colours
Of God's covenant
'We love you.'

There is no fakery
No smokescreen, no deception
Of the two-faced monkey
As I sat, just looking
Hoping that the tears would not
Pour solidly from my eyes.

Kirsty Wilkes

SOMETIMES IN THE DARK

I sit 'n' wonder
will there ever be
sometimes in the dark
I lie 'n' listen
will I ever hear
sometimes in the dark
I stand 'n' pace
will I ever move
sometimes in the dark
I cry
will you ever come.

Mercy Grace Kisinza

THE BEAUTY BEYOND THE LOOKING GLASS

What lies beyond her looking glass
Does truly a beauty make
'Tis not the mere beauty of her face
But a warmth inside her soul it takes
What lies beyond her eyes that dream
So genuinely a beauty reveal
'Tis not the colour, size nor shape
But a reflection of true compassion she feels
What lies beneath her surface shows
The gifts each beauty knows
'Tis not the tiara or gossamer gown she wears
But her humour and intuition she shares
What lies inside her heart does tell
The secrets a beauty understands so well
'Tis not what she keeps to herself each day
But the hope and charity she gives away
What lies within her vibrant spirit glows
The enchanting charms of her inner beauty
'Tis not the jewels in her bracelet, ring or lavaliere
But the blessings of grace and trust she bestows.

Jeanne Holland Newton

CROSSING THE BORDER

Crossing the border
We lost all sense of home
We just wanted to roam
Ever and ever, onwards

Crossing the line
We could never go backwards
We could only go forwards
Never to return

Crossing the barrier
We found the world a circle
There is no escape
What is behind turns towards us.

Paul Thompson

COASTAL BLUFF

Frozen laughter
Slices through salt edged air;
Squeals of delight echo incongruously,
Weaving amongst deserted chalets.
An ageless orange skyline
Remains subdued as filigree

Sunshine splinters along
Promenades carpeted with silvery hoar.
Motionless faces
Stare seawards, breathing with the tide
And isolated shores confront a
Grey, foaming aggressor:
Seemingly unannounced.

Local with a walking stick:
Standing, sideways,
Huddled beside an arcade,
With a lady who smokes
And a dog that shivers.
The rock emporium is up for sale.

Daylight suffers as a blanket of
Gloom shrouds each stranded folly;
Deep, mournful, marble shadows
Accumulate:
A lone tug-boat exhales.

Songs of summer evaporate
Into a clear, star-speckled night.
Pier: Victorian, ailing, paint peeling,
Lists just a little more,
Groaning amid the waves.

The Punch and Judy man
Stands alone on the beach:
In silhouette;
With wet feet,
Waiting.
As, just fleetingly,
He sights silence,
Drifting through dunes:
A grotesque; abandoned by time
Beneath a moon of motionless poise.

Steve Holloway

HAPPY FAMILIES

Returning home,
A balloon of enthusiasm stringed on high,
Aged habits and a derisive wall
Prick the pleasure.
Any communicating cracks are filled
With repelling force.
I retreat to my room,
Trailing shrivelled rubber
To erase the hurt by
Seeking solace in similar souls,
Strangers speaking via the ethernet
And in sending off a supporting letter
To save a threatened home.

Jean Crosbie

EARTH MOTHER

Earth Mother
Clad in gorgeous cloak
A haunting display of beauty beyond
Though dissipating wealth below.

Earth
Civilisation bashed her so hard
Industrialisation a staunch avarice
Population kept it ragged and jagged

Earth Mother
Now widowed and withered
Fertility desecrated by earthlings
Flesh cut open as sharp air prowls

Earth
Still afflicted by defiant spirits
Groans and clasps for survival
Now a silhouette of waning love

Earth Mother
Erupts with shrieking anger atop
Tears melt down flowing south
As ferocious season bares north

Earth
Watched by hopeless onlookers aside
Sacrificed for pursuit of power
Devoured by inauspicious omen.

Earth! Oh Mother Earth!

Chukwumeka Ulor

THE VINES

Gathering in shadows, waiting, breeding,
Cramming the emptiness clutter allows.
Dark tendrils gaining strength, wanting, needing,
Brooding thoughts the best library to browse.

Solitary nights a cradle to nurture,
Weary days a playground to flirt.
An army of arms send out their searcher.
Victim weakening, a mind to convert.

Surrounded by vines the windows tarnish,
Bleak lonely landscapes confuse the view.
Laughter and love become just a varnish
As memories accustom to the hue.

While vetchlings flourish on the arid grounds,
Strobing figures play out a morbid mime
Disabled and deafened by silent sounds,
Chalky orbs of hope promise to end time.

But in dreams vivid colours do run,
Each morning a small fragment left behind.
Through a kaleidoscope espied the sun.
Each shard a promise of life there to find

The choice this time is not to let them win.
Is taking your life the ultimate sin?

Judi Harvey

ANOTHER PLACE
(The Anthony Gormley Figures At Crosby)

Still here, wreathed in mist,
You look at what?
Those who are further out
Breasting the waves,
Who do not
Twist around
To see what they have left behind.

You, too, forsake the shore,
But hesitate and silent stand
In awe of that expanse,
Not knowing what you'll find.

To go where some dim future calls,
Or stay and rust away,
Embedded in the sand
For many a day,
Until at last you fall
Into the sea and drown,
Is this your fate?

Is it too late
To turn back
To your imperfect world?

Sylvia Herbert

UNTITLED

A bird sits caged for countless years

Dreaming of the Heavens.

Now free, it cannot fly.

Peter Tinsley

CRUNCHED CREDIT

I am so lucky
The crunch is not with me
Not so many millions
In excess of 1.3

Roofs have gone,
Maybe friends and gardens too
Food is so meagre
And a hole in the shoe

Families are crowded
In rooms not made for three
Young children do not
Understand economy

They say it will pass
Let's hope they are right
But just at the moment
No end is in sight

They tell us
We've been here before
But not in our time

Just give us a job
Empty pockets to line
Hope in our hearts
And a ladder to climb

To press on regardless
One step at a time.

Rita Beresford

INHERITANCE

When I was young sat upon my father's knee,
The ways of the world were made known unto me.
We were working class, of that no doubt,
Thus our place in society was already mapped out.

The ruling classes have but one aim in life,
To keep us down through war and strife.
To be working class is to be an also ran.
It has been thus since time began.

The Industrial Age finally enslaved us all,
The ruling classes had us in their thrall,
Maximising profits is the capitalist's game,
No regard for the workers to achieve their aim.

Grandmother hauled tubs from the coal seam,
She knew to escape was but a dream.
Cheaper than a pony, crouched and bent,
For the pit owner a pittance well spent.

To them the working classes have no soul.
Great Britain was built upon this bloody coal.
Remember how the Jarrow marchers of Thirties fame
Were starved into submission by the capitalist game.

Father entered the cotton weaving shed
Aged just eleven, wishing he was dead.
Inspected outside daily before work began,
Clogs, teeth, fingernails, no life for a man.

All dignity stripped, and if you failed inspection
You were sent home to do some reflection.
Why, after all you're only a hand,
Plenty more in line to enrich this land.

Kissing the shuttle will shorten your life
As cancerous oils take you or your wife.
Lose your hearing amidst that incredible din,
For the mill owner it's all the same to him.

Parliament empowered a worker's holiday,
The owners complied, but there was no pay.
So it's walk to the next mill town and stand in line,
If work is found then tonight we may dine.

Our education is never food for the mind,
Just enough to make us more useful in line.
Very carefully thought out this capitalist plot,
There's to be no escape in the workers' lot.

Pride in one's country, nationalism, it's just another ploy
Drummed into each worker from birth, each girl, each boy.
Ruling class greed is simply boundless
As other countries' wealth they seek to possess.

This greed starts wars, have no doubt
Because of it workers are mobilised and shipped out.
Win lose or draw, for them the result's the same.
It's certain they'll be working for a capitalist again.

The ruling class achieve this by playing the patriot card,
To keep them in power you may leave the mill yard.
That symbol of war, the bayonet, I tell you my friend,
At the moment of impact has a worker at each end.

'A home fit for heroes.' That's what they were told.
But on their return it's back in the cold.
Many locked out from factory and mill,
Fires kept by cinders from the slag heap hill.

Mother had rickets like many wee wains,
Iron leg callipers her very first chains.
The ruling classes were spared this disease,
Sat at high table, they ate as they pleased.

When her turn came she had no choice,
Women of those days they had no voice.
So, it's off to the mill and become a hand
Creating more profit for the rich of the land.

Clogs on cobbles are heard no more,
Cotton now woven on a cheaper capitalist shore.
For so many, the workhouse is their dismal fate
Where a friendly Grim Reaper makes his welcome date.

At my school bright working class kids had no chance,
It takes money to go to university to learn a new dance.
So when schooling's over they very soon find
It's off to the factories with the rest of their kind.

It's my turn, apprenticed, all is fine
But I'm sacked and blacklisted for not toeing the line.
It's now my turn through the door of the mill,
For the family it's hard. A bitter pill.

I'm a hand, a number. I have no name.
To the ruling class we're all the same.
Maximise profit, keep wages low, be on time,
If the workers object, put them back in the line.

Carrying huge weights out into the cold
In a job where you quickly grow old.
One day my back gives way,
Crippled for life and bills to pay.

The future is bleak if you're realistic,
After all you're just another statistic.
The path we tread has no noblesse,
For us that's just how it is.

'You've never had it so good!' That's what we were told.
It didn't feel like that as our bodies were sold.
Around this time Kathleen became my wife,
We've helped each other through troubles and strife.

Mother died, now so long ago,
Worked to an early death through men's ego.
Father died gasping for air, I see him still,
Lungs corrupted by years in the mill.

But Kathleen and I, we've fooled them this time,
We had no children to stand in their line.
No wide eyes to look up from your knee
As you tell them how it's going to be.

I am the last of my line to sit at a father's knee,
We'd have no slaves to be like you, and like me.
The hour glass is running. It's almost out of sand.
They say when I go I'm allowed my six feet of land.

David Brown
63 years of age: Ex Lancashire Mill Worker

GWLASOW

I walked again last night in the country of my dreams.
Amnesiac months, a year can pass,
But every time when I return
Nothing has changed. Even the weather is the same.
I see the everlasting hills,
Tread the footpath's springing turf,
Look down on slate-grey roofs
And swoop into the narrow lanes,
Floating past terraced, granite cottages
To the harbour and the boats.
'Take me out,' I cry, but the crew
Always say that it's too rough beyond the bar.
Don't they know that I can sail? That years ago
My parents took me on an ocean ship
To the land that's never seemed like home?
But they're right. I want to stay.
I know the place so well although
I've never seen it with my waking eyes.

Time for the duty call on my old aunt. I go
The long way round, for I shan't find her house
In its maze of Cornish streets unless I reach the fork
From where that little lane will lead me.

This time I'm here. We sit and talk,
But what we say I never can recall.
I've not seen her, nor anyone I know,
In a tiny house like this.

Did the wall dissolve?
I'm in the street again, flitting fast,
Trying to see more before the dream dissolves.
Can hauntings come not only from the past
But also from the future? Can it be
That aged aunt's myself, forgetful, worn,
The visitor some niece as yet unborn?
If that is true, I know this exile will return.

Nancy Rudden

RUMOURS

Aeons ago
In a faraway galaxy
Light years removed
From our human ken,
Joyous, contented,
Knowing no sorrows,
Dwelt on a planet
The little green men.

Happily loving
Their little green girlfriends,
Tenderly caring for
Little green babes.
Some thought they heard
Echoes from outer space
Creatures, threatening
Their little green ways.

'Nonsensical rubbish,'
Said little green leaders,
'No one out there,
'No such life can exist.'
But little green mothers
Hugged little green children
Murmuring fearfully -
'What if there is!'

Frank Hooley

SNOW

A bird
Fluttered its wings.

Atrocious
Was the snow.
Terminus
Was far away.

Poor thing,
It trembled in air.
Causing to
Go with the wind.

Still,
It fought, hushed up.

Perpetual
Was the weather.
Sempiternal
Was when it would cease.

Pathos
To its condition.
Fading into
The snow forever.

The bird was me.
The snow was grief.

Lakshmi Gopinathan

NATURE'S SEA VIEWS

Calm seas over Ramsey Bay,
Headland rocks, jutting out to sea,
Cottages nestling against green banks,
Small horizon, with clouds gathering
Just smudges, etched across the sky.
Daffodils clinging to the hedges
That meander along the lane,
Swaying gracefully in the breeze.
Rabbits, scampering over the fields,
Disappearing with a flash of white tail.
Young lambs, suckling
As their mothers stand patiently,
Then off they go leaping with joy
At the sights they may see.

Elizabeth Adams

IN THE LION'S DEN

I always know where you'll be;
So I sit there long enough
And you come to me.
And in that moment,
I'm in the limelight of your eyes;
I'm in Nirvana;
I've won every prize.
Then you dart away;
And I'm left to watch
As you work the room
Like the moon works the clocks.
And in that moment
It all becomes clear;
Trying to hold you down,
Is like trying to catch the wind
With a spear.

Rachel C Zaino

DEAD IN THE MORNING

There's a dirty light shining in the night,
That makes the whole world darker.
And blind men see what they used to be,
Which helps the nosy parker.

He looks in bins for people's sins,
And empties dirty tables.
To poke through muck and piles of stuff,
Helps spoil babies from their cradles.

I can see some more at the Cheap Jack store.
They're killing death with pleasure.
And the lie that broke when George Washington spoke,
Is filling the world with fables.

There's the dust of death and stinking breath
From open tombs in the graveyards.
So put on your paint, your eyelids' taint,
You'll all be dead in the morning.

I can't remember the score, it don't matter no more.
Old newspapers blow in the gutter.
So you spit on the floor, smash bottles some more
For you'll all be dead in the morning.

A royal family or two, a president too,
They're all on the backs of the punters.
Cos that's what we are, in the high-rise bizarre
And we'll all be dead in the morning.

Roger Penney

THE GOOD WOMAN OF BANGKOK

She came from Udon, in the north-east
A pretty Thai girl, black hair cascading down her back
The young but womanly good looks showed through
High cheekbones on her Asian face, curving lips, they could be ready to smile
Her eyes were black pools of liquid calm,
She was truly gorgeous
But unfortunate circumstances in rural life led this woman to make an untimely
decision
Money she needed, to support a daughter, help the family, pay off a father's debt
This good woman went to Bangkok, and joined the game.

Aoi sits quietly, talking softly, but with high emotion
The pain she has suffered is hinted at, in her shining damp eyes
Words of sadness and suffering come tumbling forth
Pretty features suddenly transpose an ugly snarl and,
Spitting the words out with all the venom and hatred she can muster,
Aoi declares, 'I hate men, Thai men, foreign men . . . all men.'
Her lilting, broken voice continues, 'If I had a wish, I make no men on Earth.'
The brave face cracks, emotionally overcome, Aoi seeks solace away from the
camera.

This girl's story hit me like a mortar shell of anguish, straight to my heart
What has this world done to Aoi, I ask with anger,
And incomprehension, how can it be so cruel to such a lovely girl?
I feel, and know, she has a good heart, has only tried to do right by her family
So broken now, there seems to be nothing left
The slender hope, long fled, Aoi survives only with a depression of untold depths

This woman needs to be emotionally rescued, needs the hope restored,
She needs a trusting hand to hold
Because, at this moment, she is beyond care, beyond redemption
Emotion is withered, like a dried leaf, within her soul
'I think I could not love again!' she confesses,
'I not know what it is. Money I need . . . just money.'
Her heart has hardened to a stone and,
Aoi continues the job she hates and makes her way
Trapped in the circle of self-made destiny

Aoi received help once, was given a farm and returned to the rural life
But she must have felt the cause a worthless one
Within one year, she had fled back to the city
Despite having everything that she had previously worked toward
Aoi was given a chance and still she returned to the calling

She had not asked for that help, and is not seeking any now
The woman has become machine-like, there only to provide a service
Already, she had has a lifetime of sex
'I hate them, the dirty men, the fat men, the ugly men.'

Aoi can never remember being happy, she says
Not even as a child, there is no laughter now.
Somewhere in that stony heart, a little love must surely live
I want to take her away from such an appalling life
Find that love, show Aoi how it can grow
And tell this good woman that men can respect, they can care,
And love with a heart, and not a cock.

Aoi, you tugged hard on my heartstrings, you made me cry
Someone could love you, I would love you
If you only would be willing to take a chance, to trust a little again
The sad and broken woman of Bangkok
Aoi.

Leigh Billett

THE SEA

Walking down the street,
I empty my pockets
Of the sea I was looking
After for you. Mussels
Come tumbling first.
Cracking open their castanet
Shells on the pavement.
Acres of seaweed and oysters.
Taking a deep breath,
I pour saltwater into the middle
Of the road. Islands of people
And cars bob in the newly created sea.
Somewhere amongst this
Is an old trawler. You are inside,
Sending signals back to a lighthouse
Forgotten in a trouser pocket.

Christian Ward

TROMPE L'OEIL OF TEARS

Rising out of a charged bane,
tints and shades of pouring rain.
With shine of a lasting abstain,
paints an abstract fresco of pain.

Deepened with a marking stain,
colours matching the ancient arcane.
Bounded by one glittering chain,
like the blotch of an egoistic reign.

Emblazoning the wounded sprain,
with impasto of a brushy disdain.
Priming the injury, just to sustain,
tries coating the heart but in vain.

Blanched and dried on a broken pane,
purified, rises beyond the skies twain.
Stippling Cloud Nine like a small plane,
vanishes in the myriad *tanka* domain.

Feel the daub of creation, mundane,
while sitting still in a darkened refrain.
Hiding a *pentimento* of the love vein,
emerges illuminated by Eonian again.

Sunny Kapoor

Trompe l'oeil - A painting rendered in such great detail that the viewer believes it is reality.
Charged - Saturated.
Fresco - A mural painting done with watercolours on wet plaster.
Blotch - an irregularly shaped spot.
Emblazoning - Decorating with colours.
Impasto - Painting that applies the pigments thickly, so that brush or palette knife marks are visible.
Priming - Preliminary coat of paint or sizing applied to a surface.
Blanched - Deprived of light while growing so as to turn pale.
Strippling - Applying paint in small dots or strokes.
Tanka - A Tibetan religious painting on fabric; also a style of Japanese poetry.
Daub - A blemish made by dirt; also, to brush on or smear on paint.
Pentimento - The reappearance in a painting of an underlying image that had been painted over (usually when the later painting becomes transparent with age).
Eonian - The eternal.

THROUGH THE WINDOW

Light and essence combine,
Gazing through in sombre nothingness;
Fearlessly and without remorse,
Into wavering straight light a blinding truth.

Now as it once was it is transient.
Spiral luminescence,
Towering walls of light,
Opening into a kingdom of justice and future realised.

Here the hammer falls on his right side,
Tormenting truthful but
Right; is born in mystic mind,
And faith in glass reflection.

But is it truth? Eternal . . . ?
When life slowly rots,
Representation twisted,
Stained in a distorted pane of glass,
Mouldy residue not wiped away.

Pretty puppeteers of the meek thousands,
What is right in a corrupted people
Seeing through contorted windows.
What is light;
When given off by a flickering bulb?

As it blinks,
Hiding truth,
Foresight,
Only showing what it thinks is right,
Splintering the view, cracking the glass,
Building dirty trenches on both sides.

Only when there is true light,
The heavy beating vigilant sun,
In mid-afternoon, which sits, judging,
Forcing the gloom to penance.
Will 'justice' ever be known,
Without clouding in and out of the
Consonant and vowel?
Seen through a window, whole true and right,
Not smashed,
But beautiful, glittering and bright.

Matthew Watkins

REFLECTIONS

As a child I was wrapped under innocence's arms
Like the sun under the blanket of the blue sky
Unlike every other child, taking my first step was difficult but
I let slip from the crawling era and captured the Earth's magnetism

With my own two feet - I tasted the strength of minerals under my   soul -
When I swam amongst the wealth of Earth like the roots of a tree
I merged with the amethyst, ruby, jasper, pearls, citrine and serpentine
And bloomed with glitter sprinkles on branches like a reason . . .

To satisfy the ever peckish stomach of life kind -
With the purest of seeds and fruits like the word of this moment
Humankind as ever leaned on glass and mortar for greater satisfaction
Being kind's journey was a soul search for self-knowledge and emancipation

I refused to be fused with modern society and its behaviour on its   people
Because on that land, confusion was yoked on humanity like an eclipse
They were hitting high notes in social systems like degrees and PhDs
but . . .
Failed to resolve their innate diseases that eternally deceased many

Have we been crippled by the power of the waving note upon horizon stardom?
'Cause I've seen the weak and strong, young and old on a fierce battle
The set-up has been to see who conquers a lot of this miracle pill called 'dough'
But it was a pill mistakenly consumed to bring power and never freedom

It's upon these twists and ponders that led me onto a quest
Power of 'dough' may seem like a joke and yet its attributes remain deadly
I have unclothed my spiritual suit and jumped into the staled spirits of the world
Like the company of liquor and drugs - I'm in a battle stay afloat
Abysmally sucked into the trap which I once thought brought relief
My body now lies still, cold, hard and breathless as . . .
I embark on a reflection right back to the beginning when it all started
Like paying a visit to a page left unpainted in my childhood days

George Kwarteng

TED MAD YEARS

I came into the world a soaked and clamouring babe; was washed, and then cried the indignity to the void of the unknown future.

Like a million among millions, my mind and soul grew syllable upon syllable, neuron upon neuron, growing and connecting; becoming the soft then hard, the steel then feather, the stone upon cemented stone until in a dawning, my talent breathed my words into life on a page. And like the babe in arms I was, out poured the birthing syllables: those of loss, fulfilment, fear and the deepest of souls' connection.

Now, ten years later, those words finally begin to make sense, and in their depth and significance the worlds raptures and horrors become known, and mean everything they are and will forever be . . .

. . . ten times the wheel of the world has spun, and as it spins it talks to me in the most powerful of mind-elaborating ways, like stars being born in the depths of my mind these ideas flicker into life, and I hope they will live on for an eternal time.

Ten fragments of ancient leaves fall through my fingers like the drop of sycamore seeds, and as those years fall behind as years always do, retreating, becoming the plaything of memory and life's thoughts, and so I now see a way for me to live in harmony and connection and then live to tell of no terrible toll:

Spark life in constant mind dreams I tell my mind and soul, move like a lance of lightning, and instil the daggers of the heart, leave nothing untold. That story of life and the soul it spirals endless in the mind, and in its constancy of invention there is seen the birth of a towering ethos: Like Eros I shall stride the world replete, replete, and possibly distance from those scatted myriad loves of old. But then, as I move, I move and fall like the million seeds from that very sycamore tree, and as I do so, I know that one day I will find those beatific, perfect, mind-settling lives of old.

David Finlay

TEMPTATION

Do you know how easy it is to be tempted?
The human you look at and try to meet?
Who is tempting who?
You can wait sometimes for him to see you. Waiting is the word.
The end of the bus queue you try to catch his eye.
You know he can see you, but is he seeing a space?
Are you the person he saw, but not quite, standing by his workplace?
Are you the person who trotted behind him?
He is not quite sure.
The temptation as I call it is rich and lovely, well maybe just for a little while.
You wait for that metamorphosis.
With temptation comes loneliness. Why should I be alone?
Why I am failing with this temptation, to try so hard and fail all the time?
Take the reins of this disease, slowly disappear and start again.
This temptation dies for a time but lives secretly in our thoughts until the next
                                                              time.

Darren Morley

OVER THE TOP

Out of the mist a whistle blew,
a dampened sound.
Then a shout, then more,
and shots rang out, mud spattered all around.
We leapt, adrenaline-fuelled and quick, some fell, silent; some cried out.
Noise, flurry, fire, flash, breath steaming, hearts pounding like   the guns.
Shouts no one heard, words, only words, falling like shells, bereft of their targets.
Alive; still alive and racing, slipping,
stumbling into the grey, realising;
I haven't yet fired a shot; haven't yet seen my enemy, only other men.
Terrified.
Then pain, unbelievable pain,
my shoulder gone and falling rain.
I close my eyes, all senses fade.

Tony King

UNTITLED

The sky is dark, cracked and broken,
A shower of rain comes pouring down,
Like tears showering from Heaven,
This is just a lonely town.

Depression is my one and only companion,
The one who is always there for me,
He takes my dreams and all my passion,
I feel I will never be complete.

Death and darkness are all around me,
Tears are rolling down my cheek,
I look inside and search for answers,
It is all the same week on week.

So I am left alone once again,
Crying for all I have lost,
I curl myself up and keep on sobbing,
I'm always left counting the cost.

Because nothing is left here for me,
Of all the good things that seem to happen,
None seem to happen to me.

Christopher Carpenter

PUSHING

Pushing down upon my head
The weight of life and its tread.
Negative expressions in my head,
Feelings that I so despise,
Always looking down on life,
Pulling back my will to fight.
Shaking, sweaty, trembling bones
Pull me down into the earth.
As I gasp for light and air,
Something makes me feel aware.
Life can be worth the struggles we bear
And lift us up beyond despair.

Stephen Llewellyn

THE BEAUTIFUL NOW

He's been peeking into my box
Of the beautiful now.
There he finds the word
'Rejoice'
Rejoice for the sunny day
And coloured spring things.
Rejoice for the slapping rain.
There he finds the word
'Hallelujah'
Hallelujah for the right things
That do not hurt us.
The rock foundation of happy childhood
And the other things
That help us so much.
Kind friends.
Understanding friends.
Enough money.
Our new baby girl
tied in pink ribbons.

Mary Braithwaite

AT PEACE IN THE LIGHT

Do not shed a tear for me
As I am at peace in the light.
After all it's only my physical body that has gone.
I need you to know that my spirit lives on.
For all you have to do is place just a small thought of me into your mind
And I'll be right next to you
So don't dwell or drown yourself in sorrow over me
As I am more alive than ever before
For you must remember that when it is time,
We will be at peace in the light together forever.

Tracey Marlene Celestin

SOME REDISCOVERED

Since tasting much which Man was gifted,
None so fine as verve forsaken,
Sensations stolen from their keeper,
The sweeter being, roughly taken,
One glance to fill those silent ages,
Objections hushed, and dreams be still,
For coming steady is a new light,
Mindful in our human will,
Decisions gestured through the empty,
Ambushed fate to claim this day,
Such thirst for novel, brief and hollow,
Revere the cost since none shall stay,
Only he who watches closer,
Notices what others miss,
Could be the one she'd leave this world for,
Existence paid, spent for a kiss,
This beauty stemmed from one place separate,
Felt by him that heart pierced through,
So with a draw, she grasped her knowing,
Abandoned old, fresh hope through new.

Carlene Dandy

ALL HALLOWS' EVE

From crypt black and graveyard quiet;
Spectres come in grey rot riot;
All manner of unearthly beast abroad;
In muted rage against bolted doors;
Scratching and scraping moans from Hell;
Half faces at windows of long dead shells;
All coffins lie empty all tombs lie breached;
The dead walk among the living this eve;
'Ware you who venture out on this night;
For you are the wrong and they are the right;
Lie quiet in your beds and long for the dawn;
Clutching your crucifix clutching your straws;
For death respects all equal and true;
Know one day one outside will be you.

Martin O'Toole

THE BLUEBELL GLADE

The warmth of the sun
once again on my face.
I have returned to my
very special place.
The heady scent of the
bluebells surround me,
Reminding me of times gone past.

Once again, I have stepped
off life's roller coaster,
It twists us, spins us
in every direction,
Until we no longer have
the sense to stop, reflect,
and drink in the beauty
of nature,
the purpose of life,
the importance of peace.

The stillness is interrupted
by the occasional drumming
of a woodpecker on a tree.
Sunlight glistens on the
woodland path.
Dewdrops sparkle on newly spun webs,
and for the first time in months
I feel I can breathe again.

The healing years
have been tentative and slow,
Like a shadow I can't embrace,
Unable to find a way out of the dark
and never-ending tunnel.

The light is shining now,
Birds are calling,
Trees are whispering to me,
'Walk deeper into this
Heavenly place.'
Take time to look with
New found sight.
Birds must migrate,
Gut instinct tells that they

must go,
Something is not right
where they are.
A new place must be found
In order for them to survive.

Movement, change, light,
growth and decay
are the lifeblood of nature.
We must slow down,
observe,
listen,
and marvel in its splendour.
It is only then we will
feel alive again.

Jo Storey

LOST BEGINNINGS

Long ago from lost beginnings
From a past that never fades,
Like the sun always burning
Shadows from remembered days.
Always there within the darkness
Forgotten hearts lost in time,
Tears fall deep on graves so shallow
Can you hear the beat of mine?
With the broken rise and fall
I draw breath, a sigh of pain,
Disappears through lips so silent
Words unspoken in fear of blame
A troubled heart and worried mind
Is nothing more than Satan's curse,
Turning dreams into nightmares
From good to bad, from bad to worse.
Let me sleep until it's over
Wake me up when I can breathe,
Free of pain and lost beginnings
From this Hell I want to leave.

Lisa Jane Mills

HIGH SUMMER

Dizzy heat shimmering from the Earth
Refuses its clutches.

Urban sweaty crowds lumbering
Through monotony of congregations
Halt as one at contentious lights
Pompously propped at the corner of the thoroughfare.

Traffic slurps, rambles, screeches.
The dripping masses, wide-eyed
Gaze in exasperation.

Weary labourers long for tree or hedge.
Cows trek monotonously to shade
In long low moans.
Only the ants are busy
Swarming the air with agitation.

In rural gardens all is silence;
Birds are hidden - flowers droop.
Eerie emptiness grabs our spirits
And quickly we turn to see
Who is there!

Grass is parched - trees say nought
The azure sky, inert, exists out of boredom.

Come rain, come wind, come summer.

Lesley Francis

THE MINERS LAST SHIFT

The tall sheet metal colliery gates
sound out a rattle as they close
shutting to the day-shift heel,
trudging echoes of a thousand coarse voices
reverberate the mine
ghosting like a wistful wind
where lamplit figures move
through moans of industrial machinery.
An assembly of heavy-booted hardship
toils beneath the rust of steel girder
scouring knuckles of coal
to the rhythmic pounds
of perennial digging,
urging gradual descent
to the ache of the Earth's bowel
where a stifling heat takes hold,
slowing them down long enough
to hear campaigners above ground
singing full throated from the picket line
damning the repentant closure that threatens
in protest, in vain.

Lee Severns

LESSONS FOR THE CHILD

When the sunlight hits your eyes
And the morning bids you rise:
Oh my child, lift up your head.

When the rain comes down in sheets
And runs down to your feet:
Oh my child, lift up your head.

When a stranger looks right at you
Don't let fear distract you:
Oh my child, lit up your head.

When a friend treats you with wickedness
But then comes to you for forgiveness:
Oh my child, lift up their head.

When the day is all you fear
And you end it, drenched in tears:
Oh my child, lift up your head.

When your teachers seem to hate you
And all your friends forsake you:
Oh my child, lift up your head.

When the world just seems too much to ask
And your studies drag you out to task:
Oh my child, lift up your head.

When you're in company or on your own
And either way you feel alone:
Oh my child, lift up your head.

When it doesn't make any sense
And madness pulls down your last defence:
Oh my child, lift up your head.

When someone slurs your name
And you are drowned in shame:
Oh my child, walk out the door
Your ego isn't worth losing more for.

When everything is sweet confusion
And, at that, in vast profusion:
Oh my child, let your emotions roll
They're only guides, you can control.

When you face injustice
Or face someone else's:
Oh my child, plead and fight their cause
One day it might be yours.

When you face a situation
For which there is no legislation:
Oh my child, embrace the night
Sometimes it brings the brightest light.

When only violence greets you
And they're convinced they'll beat you:
Oh my child, stay down, remain
Eventually they'll stop, and you can rise again.

When murderers and rapists take your nation
When everything's abuse and degradation:
Oh my child, subvert, rebel, resist
Choose war or peace as you see fit.

When someone else kills all you had
And you get a chance to pay them back:
Oh my child, what they did to you
Should not make you a monster too.

And when someone's actions make you sick
Destroying love and you want to quit:
Oh my child, embrace your rage
And use it to escape that cage.

And when you fall, as I know you will,
In love once more and can't stay still:
Oh my child, take the risk
Life's short, and chances pass too quick.

And when you think of something new
But are afraid to put your faith in you:
Oh my child, it's worth the try
And friends you have will stand beside.

When the beauty captures you
When the world enraptures you:
Oh my child, the heart-swell take
The wondrous organ will not break.

And when your last hour is at hand
And finally you understand:
Oh my child, lift up your head.

Jonathan Hobdell

THERE IS A PLACE

You came from among the class subjugates,
Injustice all around in your Deep South.
A boy, who felt and saw the worst of hates;
The folks in white cloaks minded Pinko north
- To Jack and Lynd it had electoral worth.
Babylon and their brimstones took a hold,
In the Johnny-Reb cap, with Yankee gold.

Your father began those fine foundations,
Yet your heart 'n' head ached for deeper core.
A college youth sensed changing relations,
Beyond Jefferson's jibes of Black-mind store;
The tear gas of spite, nooses of war.
A serenity beckoned in the shade,
'Cross cotton pickins to yo Everglade.

Coretta's love, Gandhi's inspiration,
Fuelled a vista-fresh rev's orator lot;
Gave push to higher-plain destination.
Your words were loving and prophetic hot;
Their hope to every rainbow-coloured tot.
You faced with courage the scums and shallows,
Walked on with strength for golden tomorrows.

At Montgomery, brave Rosa stood up,
In boycott of bus, you added a voice:
Awed, the old redneck drank his humbled cup;
Now, the sit-and-stand ride were multi-choice.
Stabbed and close to death, Edgar did rejoice:
The yeas and nays fast in Mammon towers,
And birds cried, then laughed, in White-House flowers.

Head above the parapet in race fights,
Together, all colours marched to Love's tune.
Resisting lies from those darkest of Whites,
You spoke of peace jumping over the Moon,
A million rays of Sun to come quite soon.
The ghettos of segregation would fall
- One's character content should prove how tall.

You had a dream of that great Promised Land,
From Seattle to Saigon, unity.
On a mountaintop clenched the meekest hand,
Did not need notes to reach out em'pity.
Inheritance assured in Earth city
But they cut you down in spring '68;
Future president - wrong . . . for rightist fate.

You were no saintly mister perfection;
(I hear humanity's freedom call)
No mortals puritan in direction.
Though plantations gone, but prison farms stall,
Thanks to the preacher, we do not now crawl.
They sky is much bad, yet there some good light.
We love you, Martin, your seer's delight.

Michael Paul Shea

UNTITLED

Sons, fathers, brothers,
daughters, mothers and sisters,
come join the uphill struggle for peace and equality.
It will take decades, centuries, probably longer than we expect.
But let us keep the faith and persist.
Co-operating and consolidating,
until our dream is achieved,
until we display and receive respect.
Discussing, discovering and enforcing.
Our remedies for ills and issues
will strengthen society's sinews.
A fire has been lit,
and a movement for positive change quickens its pace.
So accept the baton as a global revolution commences.

Jerome Teelucksingh

RISE AGAINST AND FALL

The blood that is spilt in our country's name
Is the blood of sons and families' pain,
The day their tears hit the floor
Was the day they closed his coffin door.

He did his job in every way
And was proud to be serving that day,
But when that fire came round his ears,
He fought them back despite his fears.

With sweat coming out of every pore,
This is what he joined up for,
To fight the foe that wants to see
Chaos reign in supremacy.

Through all the noise he heard a scream
And he knew what it did mean.
He put down his arms and got into action,
With dressing applied he began the extraction.

Under fire he picked his mate up,
And that's when he ran out of luck,
The iron bolt entered his side,
And this is how he finally died.

But his extraction was a success,
And we are now only one soldier less,
He laid his life down for his mate as he
Who did with the ultimate dignity.

As he flies home in his coffin borne,
Fulfilling the vow that he had sworn
Now we mourn with his family's loss
Of a soldier that will never be forgot.

Alex Roissetter

A PENNY TO SEE THE PEEP SHOW

Cartoon faces moving across my sky
like a home movie;
I close tired eyes to push them away
but they haunt my mind;
happy faces, sad faces, tearful faces,
lips mouthing my name;
familiar, faintly familiar, some skeletal
expressions breaking out.

Past, present, wishful thinking signals
to the brain to shut down
but they have logged on, not ready yet
to turn me off;
lies, half lies, bad errors of judgement
like some grotesque mob
up for rough justice for want of answers
I don't have, never did;
monstrous accusations and insinuations
fall like bird droppings
on a statue's public profile, frozen in time,
trapped in its own failings.

I hear a distant cry, an echo of centuries
in pain, anger and grief
for all private lives and personal space
relegated to speculation;
new faces, clear signals, warning off
conspirators to nightmare,
put expressions of defeat to rout, deleted
like redundant icons on a screen;
benign spirits enough to grace a totem pole,
take control, cast out
canny demons let slip past a kinder humanity
by an unforgiving hierarchy.

Eyes open, eyes shut. Sky relays to pillow
the many faces of love;
we sleep, we awaken to direct and star
in our own reality peep show.

Roger Taber

STAY AWAY FROM PEOPLE

At a tender age, thoughts were sincere,
But in younger years, with a lack of understanding,
Surrounded by a lack of humanity, would develop a worry, a fear.
Pondering smallest details of next moves,
Considering reactions, body language and facial expressions,
Things that'd naturally encumber a child,
Inducing acts of obsession, a relentless session,
A burden at that stage, not widely acknowledged

For I'd wait years to discover the great wordsmiths,
Proust, Salinger, to whom I could relate.
Perhaps not a wait, I didn't anticipate them,
Although I certainly anticipated an understanding of my leanings,
But inevitable, that with guidance our paths would meet,
My eyes fixated on the fruits of their parallel thoughts.

In reflection, the wait, with the experience was a benefit
To my learning,
My now great understanding of people,
Even if their logic does break my heart.
For years of disappointment, anxiety and questions,
Would add to the thirst, now quenched,
The sweet taste, saturated with a qualified realism,
Sadly mistaken for a dose of arrogance.

I seldom wonder what the ratio of poison to blood that
Might run through an ex-lover's stream is,
Or if lack of intelligence and a self-centred,
Somehow just existence, were the fuels that'd burn her fire,
Which would embrace me.
I'd like to see my morals, integrity, loyalty, honour and honesty
Reflected before I give my all again.

So, for today at least, I'll stay away from people.

Guy Gyngell

PLEASE LET US STAY

I am an old, a black-skinned man,
Living in a western town.
I am a beautiful brown girl,
Working in a busy office.
From all corners of the world we come
Seeking the right to freedom and to work.
Please let us stay.
Do not insist that we return
To face starvation, sickness, death.
Our customs may be strange
But we will learn. Our habits change,
And we will do what work you give.
Some will wish to keep their past alive,
Have schools and worship of their own
And some will plot revolt and death,
But most will see how great the gift of peace,
Of care for health, where no one starves to death,
Children sleep safe and in the schools
Play happily. Some will become new heroes,
Athletes, football kings. Going to work
The girls are beautiful and kind, giving their seat
To old and struggling. This is a world
Where all must have their place,
Where none destroy the growing harmonies.
Old privilege must bow to wider peace
And heart be open to receive the grace
That friendship brings, and be companions in all things.

Edward Fawcett

I REMEMBER . . .

That night at the party,
I was alone and gloomy.
He was dancing with another girl
And I . . .
My heart was broken,
All hopes were shattered
And a tear escaped
From my eye.
Just then,
Like the sun appearing
Through the dark clouds,
You came to me
And asked me to dance with you.
In a moment we were on the dance floor
Swaying to the romantic music,
Our bodies clasped together,
Our eyes fixed on each other
Suddenly you leaned forward
And kissed me,
Right on the lips.
But I didn't mind
'Cause at that time
I was falling in love with you . . .

Sudara Jayasinghe

WILLIAM WILBERFORCE

Born to a family wealthy,
Lived in the city of Hull.
Never knew what it was to be needed;
His cup had always been full.

The slave trade was rife and lucrative;
Riding the crest of a wave.
Wilberforce was strong in conviction;
Nobody should be a slave.

In passive acceptance and pity;
Not wanting to cause a big frown,
This humanitarian preacher,
Would never, never back down.

There isn't many ears that will hear
A supporter who speaks for the poor.
The industry's making some money;
It doesn't matter flouting the law.

The argument raged on for decades,
And all the fuss that it made.
He took on the law, the whole British law,
But never did stop the slave trade.

Wilf Ward

BALANCE OF THE (NOTHING) DANCE

The blood brings beat
Forms heart and steam
Vibrations rise
In confine echo.

The dance gains pace;
Enhanced pulse pounds
The timber time.
Sparking, clever clone.

Rejection rears
Against the soul
Injecting fears
Dreams become real.

Compression pain
Like falling rain
Shifts calling leaf
Repeat forms life.

I beats four walls
Listens to the whispers
Secure in the rhythm,
Lost, in the data exchange.

I move strange ways
Conforms, obeys,
Yet reject it, still.
Just for the thrill
I rejects it still.

Philip Heatley

LOSS

Loss
Is the shadow
Of love
Cast
By the white light
Of passion
Right now
At its zenith.
The raw light
Past,
There is the
Inevitability
Of shade,
The promise
Of longer,
The weight
Of my life
To bear,
But no comfort
Until dark at
Last.

John Powls

MALLOW

Long, lean, laden spurs
Of bright, pink trumpets
Lean and languish,
Shading the grass beneath,
That lace the greener
For its covering.
Above, a bee's incessant hum.
Perfect, pink promises
Waving high
Against still, blue, cloudless sky.

Greta Robinson

I AM

Vulnerability is my weakness,
Weakness is my vulnerability,
Hate is caused by frustration,
Frustration appears as a result of hate,
Fearful, I am,
Fearful, is me.

Anxiety replaced by confusion,
Confusion evokes anxiety,
The source of anger is my pain,
Pain is the basis of my anger,
Timid, I am,
Timid, is me.

Rejection is formed by situations,
Situations transform into rejection,
Suspicion evolves because of others,
Others are the cause of my suspicion,
Apprehensive, I am,
Apprehensive, is me.

Happiness is essential,
The essential I cannot find,
Searching is disappointing,
Disappointment is formed by searching,
Lost, I am,
Lost, is me.

Alicia Francois-George

ANNIE'S POEM

When 'last' is 'now' one never knows.
So many 'lasts' in life.
Later in thought one should have seen a clue
To grasp perhaps a giving opportunity.
Each 'last' becomes a small bereavement
On life's path.
The milestones on our journey
Yet how to know,
To recognise the hour?

We rush headlong and busy through the years.
Other thoughts consume us.
Work and play, love and hate,
Laughter and inevitable tears.
But 'last's we don't see, till later.
Unrecognised they pass.
Phone calls, letters, partings, postcards binned.

But if we know - what comfort would it give?
Despair, unhappiness -
How could we live in such a shadow?
Anxiously waiting for a sign of 'last'.
Impossible.

And not all 'lasts' are bad.
One can be cheered by some!
What memories should we have without them,
Good and bad?
'Lasts' can be deemed experience
Guiding us along a road
To where the final 'last' is us!

Jean Rhodes

LIBRARIES

The silent scream of millions of imprisoned words
No shelf life but universal tortuous volumes of
Constrained and restrained prisoners of printed thought,
Struggles of frustrated expression needing exposure,
Now muted incarcerated and awaiting a reading audience.
Then short-term release, paroled and perused at leisure,
With those who would attempt a journey of communication
By trawling through the writer's intellect and imagination
Astride the pen and within the printed page
Perusing the pain with silent attention
Panoramic colour-filled hopes, ideas and dreams
Experiencing adventure, aspirations
Within the lives of others
Life, hate, pain and love, all together, hand in glove
Sentenced to writing sentences, for life
The writer's lot . . . paragraphs, prose and plot
Easy to do, it's not chapter, verse, smile and curse
Chapter end and stop . . .
Content without contentment
Frustration and resentment
With inspiration atip the pen . . .
Book finished, but what then?
Manuscripts' repeated rejection
Author's total dejection
But for you reader . . . it's easy
Turn the page, touch the sage, and do it at your own leisure
The writer's job once done is to give you pleasure
Now with our imagination stimulated
With scenes pen-painted with deft touch
Give of yourself liberal thoughts, authors deserve this much
Prologue to epilogue, book at an end.

Silent scream the words . . .

Alan Grainger

PHOTO OF MARILYN MONROE IN A BOOK STORE

She is cool
In black satin
Like a modern
Lady Macbeth
Or Ophelia
Blue eyes full
Of tragedy
Turning
A paperback carousel
Of love and violence
Hair bleached
From another day
Of California sun
Adolescents
Finger comic books
Unaware they stand
Shoulder to shoulder
With a legend.

Paul Wilkins

A LOVE THAT'S FOREVER NEAR

When dawn's first gleam of golden glow
Burgeons in the eastern sky
And its luminous lights the darkness
Of the night doth put to flight.

When sleep her cradling arms do me unfold
'Tis then across the yawning gulf of time
Flooding the corridors of my mind
Come those marvellous memories of all those years
Of your wonderful love and care.

That brings the tears I cannot stem
And I weep that you are now and forever gone
And yet in my lonely heart
You are forever dear and forever near.

Victor William Lown

HOPE

Cracks in the ceiling
Damp walls all around
Huddled in a corner trying to keep warm
The smell of perspiration
Through days of wearing the same old clothes
Bony fingers hold a single crust
The only remains of what a pigeon has left

The wind howls
And the rain pours
And still he begs for more

The little cap is empty
No coins have tinkled into its soft material

How long will he sit and beg?
And how many people will just walk by?

The snow has started to fall
And still he sits
Not moving a muscle
Just waiting for the joyful tinkle
Of coins falling into the soft cap

The light is fading
Doors are being shut and curtains drawn
And still he sits upon the lawn

Morning has dawned
And all that is left of the lonesome figure
Is a frozen statue of poverty on the lawn
And an empty cap waiting to be worn.

Zena Samuels

FAMILY TREE

Three weeks after he died,
My daughters came,
Bringing with them an apple tree
To plant in the garden.

It was called a family tree
Because there were three different
Varieties of fruit
Grafted onto the main stem.

Throughout the year, I watched it grow.
In the spring, the tree was covered
In delicate pink and white blossom.
Later the leaves unfurled,
Revealing the embryo apples.
Some fell to the ground,
Too small and bitter for the birds.

But it did well, and,
By the autumn,
The little tree was heavily laden,
Its branches bent under the weight of
The crimson and gold fruit.
One branch in particular,
Almost touched the ground.
I'll prop that up in the morning I thought.

That night a strong wind blew,
And the next morning found the branch
Severed from the main stem
And the fruit spilled across the dew-soaked grass.

Joy Staley

DON'T LIVE IN A TOO SMALL WORLD

We live insulated from the world
In our 'little boxes'
No dust or wind can enter
Past the double glazing

No hawker can penetrate
The iron gates or big oak door
So who can come in?
Our trusted family and friends

But is that enough to sustain us?
What about the elderly and frail?
Those without family near?
Those we find difficult?

We might fix our eyes on the pavement
Read the paper when on the bus
Ignore the phone when we are busy
Ignore those present by watching TV

But sometimes we can take courage
And offer hospitality
To those we feel might need us
In fact they well might feed us!

Barbara Tozer

CONCRETE EVIDENCE

The undiscovered
Hidden and covered
Waiting to unleash the truth
The key to the answer
The core of the cancer
Real undisputable proof.

So crucially relevant
Proving lawful impediment
The final link to incriminate
Will remain never found
Deeply buried in ground
Where they built the new housing estate.

Allison Morrell

FORWARD PRESS INFORMATION

We hope you have enjoyed reading this book
- and that you will continue to enjoy it in the
coming years.

If you like reading and writing poetry drop us a
line, or give us a call, and we'll send you a free
information pack.

Alternatively if you would like to order further copies
of this book or any of our other titles, then please
give us a call or log onto our website at
www.forwardpress.co.uk.

Forward Press Information
Remus House
Coltsfoot Drive
Peterborough
PE2 9JX
(01733) 890099